THE WEALTH WITHIN

How to Unlock the Hidden Fortune Your Mind Has Been Holding Back

Suraj Raina

Author of FMCG Blueprint

This book is for educational and informational purposes only. It does not constitute financial, legal, or therapeutic advice. Seek qualified professional guidance for decisions specific to your situation.

First published 2026

linkedin.com/in/surajraina06

For everyone who knows more than they are acting on.

"The cave you fear to enter holds the treasure you seek"

- *Joseph Campbell*

"Doing well with money is not about what you know. It is about how you behave"

- *Morgan Housel*

"Until you make the unconscious conscious, it will direct your life and you will call it fate"

- *Carl Jung*

CONTENTS

PART 3: ACTIVATE YOUR WEALTH

PART 4: BUILD WEALTH FOR LIFE

ACKNOWLEDGMENTS

Books are written alone but they are not built alone. This one owes debts that cannot be fully accounted for here.

To the distributors, sales managers, territory executives, and business owners I worked alongside at ITC, Perfetti Van Melle, Marico, and Kenvue: I learned more about human financial behaviour from watching you navigate your professional and personal lives than from any research paper. The patterns in this book are yours as much as mine.

To the researchers whose work forms the scientific backbone of these pages: Daniel Kahneman, whose framework for thinking about thinking changed how I understand every decision I observe. Morgan Housel, whose clarity about the psychology of money set the standard this book is reaching toward. Sendhil Mullainathan and Eldar Shafir, whose scarcity research named something I had been watching without being able to explain. Brad and Ted Klontz, whose money script framework gave me the language for Chapter Seven.

To my family (parents and spouse – Ankita), who have been patient with the particular quality of distraction that comes from having a book in progress. And to everyone who reads this: the wealth is within reach. It always has been.

A NOTE BEFORE WE BEGIN

Let me begin with a confession, because this book will ask you for honesty, and it would be dishonest not to offer some in return.

Early in my career, during a stretch when I was working as a sales manager at ITC, I used to sit at a tea stall between market visits and run mental arithmetic on my own finances. I was covering a dense patch of retail outlets, managing a distributor whose trust I was still earning, and hitting monthly targets that felt ambitious in the way only first jobs can. I was, by most reasonable measures, doing all right.

What I was not doing was anything with the money. It arrived. It left. The investment account I fully intended to open existed only as a recurring intention and, for a while, as three browser tabs I had researched and never acted on.

The irony was not lost on me even then. My job was to understand why people bought things, what emotional and psychological mechanisms drove a purchasing decision, why a price of ninety-nine cents outperformed one dollar not because of arithmetic but because of how the mind encodes numbers, why a consumer chose one brand over another despite identical functional performance. I was studying human decision-making professionally. And I could not make one sound financial decision for myself.

This is the paradox that eventually became this book. The gap between knowing and doing in personal finance is not a gap in information. Most people who struggle financially are not uninformed. They know about compound interest. They know that high-interest debt is expensive. They know that a salary negotiation would probably go better than they fear. The gap is not in the knowing. It is in something else entirely, something more internal, more habitual, and ultimately more addressable.

I spent the decade that followed crossing that territory in both my professional and personal life.

At Perfetti Van Melle, leading a sales team through a difficult restructuring period. At Marico and Kenvue, working on regional strategy and customer development at scale. Across every role, the most interesting thing I observed was not the commercial data. It was the

human behaviour behind it: the way intelligent professionals made sharp decisions in their work and muddled ones in their own financial lives, often simultaneously, without seeming to notice the contradiction.

What I learned from that observation, combined with the research I have read voraciously and the honest examination of my own patterns, is what this book contains. It is not a prescription. I am not a licensed financial advisor, and nothing here should substitute for professional guidance on your specific situation. What I offer instead is a map of the internal territory: the specific psychological and neurological landscape that sits between financial knowledge and financial action, described clearly enough that you can actually navigate it.

You will find science in these pages, because the science is real and illuminating. You will find stories, because stories are how humans actually learn. You will find practical tools, because understanding without a path forward is just philosophy.

The wealth is not missing. It is not locked behind a credential you lack or an advantage you were not born with. What has been blocking it is a set of patterns. Patterns are changeable. That is the whole premise, and the reason this is worth your time.

Let us begin.

The personal story above contains a broader point worth making explicit that is worth making explicit before we go further. The knowing-doing gap I experienced with my own finances was not a unique failure. It is the defining financial challenge of our time. not market volatility, not insufficient savings rates, not inadequate financial products. The gap between what people know they should do and what they actually do. That gap costs more, in aggregate, than all the bad investment decisions combined. And it is almost never addressed directly, because most financial guidance operates on the assumption that the problem is informational. Provide the right information, it assumes, and the behaviour will follow.

The behaviour does not follow. It has not for decades, despite the proliferation of financial media, education, and tools. The gap persists

because its source is not informational. This book is built on that understanding.

This book is structured for a specific reason. Part One establishes what the opportunity actually is: the concrete, calculable wealth within your reach that your patterns have not yet allowed you to access. You need to know what is at stake before the subsequent work makes sense.

Part Two examines the specific internal mechanisms blocking access to that wealth. You need to understand the patterns before you can change them. Part Three gives you the practical tools to change those patterns, designed specifically around how the nervous system actually changes. Part Four addresses the long game: how to hold what you have built, navigate disruption, and sustain financial momentum through the full complexity of a real life.

Read it in order the first time. The sequence is deliberate. Each section depends on the one before it.

That is the expertise I am bringing to this subject. Not the expertise of a financial professional, I am not one, and this book is not a substitute for professional financial advice. The expertise of someone who has spent a career studying the gap between knowing and doing in human behaviour, and who eventually turned that lens, with some overdue seriousness, on his own financial life.

Financial behaviour has an identical gap, and it is just as interesting and just as important. People say they intend to invest. They do not invest. They say they know they should negotiate. They do not negotiate. They say the debt is a priority. They pay the minimum. The gap between stated financial intention and revealed financial behaviour is not random. It is structured. It has causes. And causes, unlike random variation, can be addressed.

Most consumer research, if taken at face value, would lead to product decisions that fail in market. Consumers say they prioritise health. They buy convenience. They say they will pay more for quality. They buy on price promotion. They say they have no brand loyalty. They reach for the same product every week. Understanding the difference between what people say and what they do, and, more importantly, understanding why the gap exists and how to design around it, is the core competency of effective consumer goods strategy.

One observation from my years in FMCG keeps returning that I return to often when I think about financial behaviour. In consumer goods, we talk constantly about the difference between a stated preference and a revealed preference. A stated preference is what a consumer says they will do when asked. A revealed preference is what they actually do when given the choice. The gap between them is the most interesting and commercially important territory in the industry.

THE FORTUNE ALREADY INSIDE YOU

Why your financial problem is not what you think it is — and why that is the best possible news

"Within you right now is the power to do things you never dreamed possible"

- *Maxwell Maltz*

In 2014, a ninety-two-year-old man named Ronald Read died in Brattleboro, Vermont and left behind an estate worth approximately eight million dollars.

He had spent his career sweeping floors and pumping petrol. He wore flannel shirts and drove an old car. He shopped at used-clothing stores and fixed his own coat with safety pins. His neighbours had no idea. His lawyers had no idea. The hospitals he left his fortune to had no idea. The fortune was entirely hidden, hidden inside decades of quiet, consistent, automated investing in companies he understood and held without flinching.

Ronald Read did not have exceptional income. He did not have access to financial expertise or sophisticated investment products. What he had was the behavioural capacity to do the right thing for a long time. Morgan Housel told this story in The Psychology of Money, and it has become the most cited example in contemporary financial writing precisely because it overturns every conventional assumption about what wealth-building requires. It does not require spectacular income. It does not require genius. It requires the specific psychological capacity to keep doing the un-dramatic thing, month after month, while the world generates excellent reasons to stop.

This book is about the gap between knowing what Ronald Read did and being able to do it. Because almost every financially literate person who hears his story understands the principle immediately. Very few of them are living it. Not because they are less intelligent or less motivated than Ronald Read, but because something specific is blocking the translation of principle into practice. That something is what this book examines.

The Paradox at the Centre of This Book

Personal financial information has never been more accessible. Books, podcasts, apps, short-form videos, financial influencers, free investing platforms: the basic knowledge of how to build wealth is saturating every medium simultaneously. And yet the gap between what working professionals know and what they actually do with their money remains stubbornly, consistently wide.

Survey after survey of working adults across developed economies produces the same result: high levels of financial knowledge, significantly lower levels of financially productive behaviour. People who can correctly explain compound interest and still have not started a retirement account. People who know that credit card debt at twenty-two percent interest is expensive and still carry balances month after month. People who know exactly what they should be doing and, year after year, are not doing it.

This gap cannot be closed by more information. If information were sufficient, it would have closed by now. The gap exists because its cause is not informational. It is neurological and psychological, rooted in the structure of the human brain, the weight of inherited financial beliefs, and the self-reinforcing loops of avoidance that develop over years of not engaging with what is uncomfortable. Those causes require different solutions than the ones most financial books offer.

That is why this book begins not with a budgeting system or an investment strategy, but with a question: why do capable, intelligent, financially literate people consistently fail to act on what they already know? The answer to that question is more useful than any spreadsheet, because it addresses the actual source of the problem rather than its symptoms.

What Is Actually at Stake

Before we go any further, I want to make the opportunity concrete, because abstract financial encouragement is easy to dismiss and specificity is harder to ignore.

The average mid-career professional has five sources of financial opportunity their current patterns have not yet allowed them to access. The compounding returns foregone during the 16 years between when they first told themselves they would start investing and when they actually began. The compensation gap from salary negotiations consistently deferred, a gap whose tenyear financial impact, due to the compounding effect of a higher salary base on every future raise and job offer, is typically far larger than the individual feels comfortable calculating. The structural inefficiency of unused tax provisions and uncaptured employer matching contributions. The drag of high-interest debt being serviced slowly rather than aggressively cleared. And the behavioural compound: the multiplier effect that each small financial improvement has on every subsequent one.

Add those five sources together for a typical professional in their thirties or forties, and the figure that results is almost always larger than they estimated before calculating it. We will do your specific version of this calculation in Chapter Four, and I ask you to approach it with honesty. The number is not a verdict. It is a map of what is still available. More importantly: all of it is still available. The past is fixed. Every year of the working life ahead of you is not. Each year of good financial behaviour, started now and sustained consistently, compounds in your favour with exactly the same power it has been compounding against you.

Four Things That Block the Path

In more than a decade of working with sales teams, distributors, and business professionals, and in the honest examination of my own financial history, I have come to understand the knowing-doing gap through four specific mechanisms. Understanding all four is necessary because most financial blocks are not a single problem but an interaction between several.

The first is the threat response. When financial engagement activates the brain's threat-detection system, analytical capacity drops, long-term thinking goes offline, and the impulse to disengage becomes more powerful than the intention to act.

This is not a metaphor. It is measurable physiology, and it explains why the salary conversation that was fully prepared and rehearsed still does not happen, why the investment account that was researched for two months still was not opened, why intelligent people make poor financial decisions precisely when the stakes are highest. We examine the neuroscience in Chapter Two.

The second is inherited belief: the money scripts absorbed before we were old enough to evaluate them, operating below conscious awareness, quietly shaping what feels possible, what feels threatening, and what feels like something that other people do but not us.

These scripts do not automatically update when income increases. A person who grew up in financial precarity can earn a professional salary for a decade and still carry the nervous system of someone who might run out of money next month. Chapter Seven covers this territory.

The third is behavioural pattern: the self-reinforcing loops of avoidance and relief that develop over years of not engaging with financial discomfort. Each time you close the banking app because the numbers produce anxiety, the brain records a lesson: disengagement worked. Lessons, repeated enough times, become automatic. By the time most people recognise the avoidance pattern in their financial life, it has been running for years and has developed the kind of automaticity that information alone cannot override. Chapters Five and Six address this.

The fourth is what I call the velocity problem. Compound growth is extraordinary over twenty years and invisible over twenty weeks. In a world saturated with immediate feedback, the extended time horizon of meaningful wealth-building feels abstracted to the point of unreality. The brain, which evolved for immediate consequences, consistently undervalues actions whose results will not be visible for a decade. Chapter Eight examines this specifically.

These four mechanisms interact and amplify each other. The threat response deepens avoidance. Inherited belief strengthens the threat response. Avoidance disguises itself as rational caution. The velocity problem supplies a constant stream of plausible justifications for delay. Together, they form a system that is remarkably effective at keeping wealth just out of reach, regardless of income, intelligence, or intention.

How This Book Is Different

Most personal finance books operate primarily in what Daniel Kahneman calls System Two: the deliberate, analytical, slow-thinking mind. They provide information, frameworks, and calculations that are useful when System Two is engaged and in control.

Right now, in offices and homes across the world, this conversation is happening in offices and homes across the world. Competent, educated, motivated professionals sitting on top of an opportunity they cannot quite access. Not because the opportunity requires anything they do not have. Because the patterns between them and the opportunity have been running so long and so automatically that they feel less like patterns and more like reality.

One of the most important findings in behavioural economics, confirmed repeatedly across Kahneman's research and the decades of work that followed, is that most of the decisions shaping our financial lives are not made through deliberate analysis. They are made through automatic pattern recognition, through rapid intuitive responses that precede conscious thought.

Understanding this changes the frame for everything that follows. If financial decisions are being avoided not through deliberate choice but through automatic pattern, then the solution is not to make better choices in the traditional sense. It is to understand and modify the patterns themselves. That is a different kind of project. It takes a different kind of tool. And it produces a different, more durable, kind of change.

The financial life on the other side of that work is not a dramatic transformation. It is something more quietly significant: a financial life that is actually working. One in which the investment happens without requiring monthly heroism. One in which the salary reflects market rate because the conversation was had. One in which an unexpected expense is an inconvenience rather than a crisis. One in which the running sum of small, consistent, automated decisions is compounding, month by month, into something real. That is what is available.

That is what this book is about. The problem is that the patterns blocking most people's financial behaviour operate primarily in System One: the fast, automatic, emotionally driven mind that acts before conscious thought has formed. A book that talks to System Two about a problem that lives in System One is, at some level, talking to the wrong audience.

This book talks to both. The science is here because understanding what is happening changes the experience of it. The practical tools are here because understanding alone does not produce behaviour change. And the structure moves deliberately from why (Parts One and Two) to how (Part Three) to sustained (Part Four), because that is the actual sequence in which behavioural change happens, and any book that jumps directly to the how without establishing the why is offering solutions to people who have not yet fully seen the problem. A note on numbers: the figures in this book are illustrative. Your income is different, your cost of living is different, your tax environment is different. Where I describe financial products or tax provisions, the equivalent in your country applies. The psychological patterns this book addresses are universal. Their financial expressions are local.

Read Part One with a notebook nearby. Chapter Four is a practical exercise whose output you will use throughout Part Three. Read Part Two with as much honest self-examination as you can bring. And read Part Three as a practitioner, not a student. The tools there are meant to be used, not studied.

One last note on how to use this book most effectively. Some chapters will resonate immediately and viscerally, you will recognise yourself in them, your specific pattern, your specific cost. Others will feel less directly relevant, less urgent. Do not skip the less urgent ones.

The patterns in this book interact with each other, and understanding the ones that feel peripheral to your primary pattern often illuminates the primary pattern in ways that direct examination does not. Read it through. Then return to the chapters that are most directly relevant to where you are.

Part Four addresses what most financial books skip entirely: the long game. Not just how to start but how to sustain. How to navigate the disruptions that are inevitable in any life long enough to build significant wealth. How to return to the practice after a period when it has slipped. How to define, in personal and specific terms, what a financially successful life actually looks and feels like for you, because without that definition, there is no north star for the work, and practices without a north star tend to drift.

Part Three is where the work becomes practical. Each chapter in this section contains tools designed not for a hypothetical rational actor operating under ideal conditions, but for a real person managing real complexity, job pressures, family obligations, competing priorities, and the full complement of the behavioural patterns Parts One and Two have described. The tools work with the brain you have, in the life you are actually living, rather than requiring a life you would need to construct before you could begin.

The chapters in Part One are designed to make the opportunity concrete. By the time you reach Part Two, you will have a specific understanding of the wealth available to you and the specific calculations that make the gap between current and potential trajectory visible.

Part Two then examines the internal territory: the specific psychological and neurological mechanisms that have been creating and maintaining that gap.

A Map of What Follows

The science supports the journey. The journey is the point. Everything that matters starts here.

Part 1

DISCOVER YOUR WEALTH POTENTIAL

What is already available to you — and what has been keeping it out of reach

1.1 The Hidden Fortune

What is already available to you — and what has been keeping it out of reach

"Within you right now is the power to do things you never dreamed possible"

- Maxwell Maltz

Howard Schultz was rejected by two hundred and seventeen investors before he found the capital to build Starbucks.

Not twenty-seven. Not seventy. Two hundred and seventeen. He was trying to sell the idea of a premium coffee experience at a price point most people thought was absurd, in a country where coffee was fifty cents at a diner counter, and the people he was asking had entirely rational objections. They looked at the available evidence and concluded the risk was not worth taking. What Schultz had that the investors did not was a longer time horizon and a willingness to act on a vision that was not yet visible. He mortgaged his house. He borrowed from friends. He endured years of financial uncertainty that most people would have found intolerable, and he endured it because he could see something that had not yet become real. I am not suggesting that the path to financial security involves founding a coffee empire. What I am pointing at in Schultz's story is a principle that applies to every professional at every income level: there is wealth within your reach that is not yet visible to you, and the primary reason it is not visible has nothing to do with whether it is real. The wealth is real. It is hidden by patterns. Patterns, unlike circumstances, are changeable.

The Distributor Who Could Not See His Own Numbers

Early in my career at ITC, I managed a territory that included a distributor I will call Vikram. not his name, but his pattern is real. Vikram ran a distribution business that would have impressed any logistics professional. He had a team of twenty, managed inventory across multiple product categories, and understood his market with the intuitive fluency of someone who had spent two decades walking the same streets and building the same relationships.

When we sat down to review his numbers, his analysis was sharp. He could tell you the credit terms he was extending to any given retailer, the working capital cycle that created, and whether the margin justified it. He was, in his professional domain, a financially sophisticated operator.

One afternoon, waiting for a retailer who was perpetually late, I asked him casually what he was doing with the cash that had been accumulating in his business account over a good year. His answer has stayed with me: 'I keep meaning to look into that. It's on the list.'

The list. I had heard about the list before. The list is where financial intentions go to wait indefinitely while everything else feels more immediate.

Vikram was not unsophisticated. He was compartmentalised. The same brain that managed his business with analytical confidence operated in a completely different mode when the subject turned to his personal finances. There, he was hesitant, slightly avoidant, and quietly ashamed of being both. The gap between his professional competence and his personal financial behaviour was not a gap in knowledge. It was a gap in something else entirely, something more internal, more habitual, and more addressable.

Four years later, by chance, I ran into him at a trade event. He had, somewhere in the intervening period, stopped waiting for the right moment and started a regular automated investment. Small at first. Gradually larger. He was not wealthy in any dramatic sense. But he was building something, and the particular quality of quiet pride he had when he mentioned it: the slightly embarrassed satisfaction of someone who wishes they had started sooner but is genuinely glad they started at all, is the same quality I have seen in every person who has moved from intention to action in their financial life.

The Five Sources of Hidden Wealth

The opportunity available to most mid-career professionals is not abstract. It organises itself into five calculable sources. Understanding each one separately is useful because each has a different mechanism and requires a different intervention.

The first and most powerful is compounding not started. The mathematics of compound growth reward starting early and penalise delay with a severity that most people do not fully internalise until they see their own numbers. A modest regular investment begun at twenty-five grows to a dramatically different figure by retirement than the identical investment begun at thirty-five. not primarily because of the additional contributions, but because of the additional decade of returns on returns. Every year of delay has a specific, calculable cost. For most professionals who have been deferring, that cost is larger than they have ever explicitly confronted.

The second source is compensation unclaimed. Linda Babcock and Sara Laschever's research on salary negotiation found that professionals who negotiate consistently earn substantially more over a career than those who don't, and that the ten-year impact of even a modest salary improvement is typically several times the annual figure, because every subsequent raise and job offer is calculated from a higher base. The negotiation conversation that feels too risky to have has a financial cost that compounds every year it is deferred. We examine this in detail in Chapter Fourteen.

It is worth understanding why the hidden fortune stays hidden, why the gap between current and potential trajectory is so consistently invisible to the person experiencing it. There are three reasons, and they work together.

The first is that the costs are defined by absence. When you make a bad investment, it shows up on your statement. When you pay a penalty, there is a charge. When you do not make an investment, nothing appears anywhere. Foregone compounding has no line item. The salary not negotiated two years ago does not register as a cost. The tax provision not utilised returns nothing to signal it existed. Invisible costs are the easiest to leave unaddressed, because they generate no visible distress signal.

The second reason is the emotional dimension of financial self-assessment. Looking honestly at the gap between where you are and where you could have been requires a degree of selfexamination that activates the threat response we examine in Chapter Two. The assessment is uncomfortable not because the numbers are catastrophic but because they implicate choices, or the consistent absence of choices, that feel as though they say something about your character. So the assessment gets avoided. And the avoidance of the assessment is itself part of the pattern that perpetuates the gap.

The third reason is that the comparison point is wrong. Most people assess their financial position by comparing it to where they were last year, or to where peers appear to be. The more useful comparison, the one that makes the hidden fortune visible, is between the current trajectory and the potential trajectory: between what the mathematical reality of your income and time horizon says you could build, and what you are currently building.

That comparison requires calculation. Calculation requires honest financial engagement. Honest financial engagement is what the patterns we examine in Part Two have been reliably preventing. This is why Chapter Four is a practical exercise with your specific numbers rather than a conceptual discussion. The hidden fortune does not become motivating until it becomes visible. Making it visible requires doing the calculation, which requires sitting with the discomfort that the calculation produces. That discomfort is worth moving through. On the other side of it is the clearest possible answer to the question that sustains financial practice over years: why does this actually matter? The third source is structural inefficiency: the taxes overpaid because available provisions were never properly utilised, the employer matching contributions not fully captured, the insurance products poorly configured. This source is less visible than the others but often surprisingly large, and it is the most purely mechanical: it requires not a behavioural transformation but one meeting with a qualified professional who asks the right questions.

The fourth source is debt drag. For anyone carrying highinterest consumer debt, every month it runs is a month that a portion of their income produces no wealth whatsoever, it simply pays for the privilege of yesterday's spending. The guaranteed return of eliminating twenty-percent debt is better than the expected return of most investments. Yet most people carrying expensive debt address it at the minimum payment pace, which is the slowest and most expensive pace available.

The maths of this are available to everyone. What is not universally available is the understanding of why the changes have not already been made, and the specific tools to make them. The rest of this book is dedicated to providing both.

Think of a professional who is thirty-two years old, earning a mid-career salary, carrying a moderate level of consumer debt, and not yet investing consistently. Address all five sources over the next five years, establish consistent investment, negotiate compensation to market rate, optimise tax structure, clear the expensive debt, and let the behavioural compound begin to operate, and the trajectory from that point forward is dramatically different from the current one. Not because anything extraordinary has happened.

Because five ordinary, available, achievable changes have been made and sustained.

Viewing the five sources together matters as much as understanding each one together rather than in isolation. Each one is meaningful individually. Combined and compounding simultaneously, they represent a figure that most professionals find genuinely surprising when they calculate it for the first time.

The Compound Effect of All Five Together

The fifth source is what I consider the most important in the long run, though it is the hardest to quantify: behavioural compound. Each improved financial habit makes the next one easier. The person who starts a regular automated investment has changed their relationship with investing in a way that makes the next decision, to increase the contribution, to open a second account, to review the allocation, more accessible. The person who has one successful salary negotiation has changed something about their professional self-conception that makes the next one more likely. Behaviour improves behaviourally, and the compounding of that improvement over years is genuinely transformative.

The Reframe That Unlocks Everything

The number that ultimately matters most is the simplest one: the difference between your current financial trajectory and your potential one. That difference is the hidden fortune this chapter is named for. Chapters Four through to the end of this book are about reaching it.

I ask you to do those calculations honestly, and to hold the resulting numbers not as evidence of failure but as evidence of what is still available. The compounding delay cost is the cost already paid. The compounding opportunity from today forward is the wealth still entirely within reach. The salary gap represents money not yet earned from this employer. but it also represents the specific, calculable benefit of a conversation that could happen this quarter.

Some of those calculations will be uncomfortable. The compounding delay cost is the difference between what your investment horizon would have produced if you had started when you first told yourself you would, and what it will produce starting now. It carries the weight of real time already passed.

Throughout Part One, I will be asking you to calculate things. Not in the spirit of a financial planning exercise, we are not producing a comprehensive financial plan. In the spirit of making visible what has been invisible: the specific, real cost of the current pattern, expressed in numbers that belong to your life rather than to a hypothetical example.

The Beginning of the Calculation

Standard personal finance guidance is deficit-framed. It tells you what you are not doing, how far behind you are, and what a responsible adult would already have sorted out. The emotional register is one of mild to moderate inadequacy, and the implicit message is that your failure to have built significant wealth by now reflects something about your discipline, your priorities, or your character.

This framing is not merely unkind. It is neurologically counterproductive. Research in motivational psychology consistently shows that shame-based motivation produces short, reactive bursts of action: the frantic late-night budgeting session that generates a plan and a resolution that is abandoned within a fortnight. It does not produce the sustained, consistent, yearslong engagement that wealth-building actually requires.

What produces that kind of engagement is approach motivation: moving toward something genuinely desired rather than away from something aversive. The professional with a clear, specific, personally meaningful vision of what financial security looks like for them is a fundamentally more effective financial actor than the professional motivated primarily by anxiety about where they currently stand.

The wealth is not missing. It is not locked behind a credential you lack or an advantage you were not born with. It is in the gap between what you have been doing and what you are capable of doing.

This is the frame this book operates from throughout. Not: here is what fear has cost you. Rather: here is what is still available to you. Not: you have been failing to do the obvious. Rather: the patterns that have been blocking you are specific, understandable, and changeable, and the wealth they have been blocking is still there.

The hidden fortune is real. The chapter that follows will explain precisely why it has stayed hidden. The chapters after that will show you how to reach it.

1.2 The Brain's Wealth Blockers

Why intelligent, capable people consistently leave money on the table

"Between stimulus and response there is a space. In that space is our power to choose our response"

- Viktor Frankl

In the autumn of 2008, as the global financial crisis reached its worst point, Warren Buffett published an op-ed in the New York Times with a title that most readers found either visionary or delusional: 'Buy American. I Am.'

The Dow had fallen forty percent from its peak. Banks were failing. Economists were openly debating whether the world was heading for a second Great Depression. Ordinary investors were watching retirement accounts that had taken decades to build lose a third of their value in months. Fear was not an irrational response. It was the entirely understandable response of a nervous system doing exactly what it was designed to do.

Buffett was buying.

Not because he knew the market had bottomed, he said explicitly he had no idea. Not because he was fearless, he was not claiming immunity from the same anxiety everyone else was experiencing. He was acting from a framework: he understood what he owned, he understood roughly what it was worth over a long time horizon, and the market's short-term panic was creating prices so far below that worth that the rational response, in his framework, was obvious.

Most investors in 2008 did not share Buffett's framework. Most of them sold. Many sold at the exact worst moment, locking in real losses and positioning themselves to miss one of the largest recoveries in market history. Within three years, the market had returned to its pre-crisis levels. Within five, it had substantially exceeded them. The investors who held, through courage, conviction, or fortunate inertia, were rewarded. Those who acted on the fear were not.

This is not a story about Buffett's analytical genius. It is a story about the relationship between the human brain and financial decision-making under stress. And that relationship, once understood clearly, explains with precision why intelligent people consistently make financial decisions that work against their own long-term interests.

Two Systems and the Wealth Problem

Daniel Kahneman, whose decades of research earned him the Nobel Prize in Economics in 2002, mapped the human mind as two systems operating simultaneously. System One is fast, automatic, emotional, and associative: the mind that reacts before you have consciously formed a thought. System Two is slow, deliberate, analytical, and effortful: the mind capable of evaluating a compound interest calculation or constructing a ten-year financial plan.

Financial decisions, optimally made, require System Two. They require the kind of long-term analysis, cost-benefit evaluation, and patient reasoning that System One is constitutionally incapable of performing. The problem is that money, for most people, through years of accumulated experience, carries emotional weight that activates System One before System Two has had a chance to engage.

The banking notification that arrives on a stressful Tuesday is not emotionally neutral. The number on the investment account screen during a market downturn is not emotionally neutral. The salary conversation with a manager you see every day is not emotionally neutral. These stimuli carry charge, learned charge, built from years of experience in which financial events were accompanied by stress, conflict, inadequacy, or fear. When that charge is sufficient, System One takes the wheel before System Two has started the engine.

This is why financial education alone so rarely produces financial behaviour change. Education informs System Two. The blockages live in System One. You can understand compound interest at a genuine intellectual level while simultaneously experiencing, in your body, a threat response every time you try to act on that understanding. The understanding and the block coexist because they live in different systems.

The Amygdala: Your Brain's Security Guard

At the centre of System One's threat-detection architecture sits the amygdala, a small almond-shaped structure whose primary function is to identify danger and mobilise a response. It is extraordinarily fast, research suggests it activates threat responses in approximately twelve milliseconds, well before conscious awareness has formed, and it is extraordinarily powerful. When the amygdala fires, it initiates a biochemical cascade: cortisol and adrenaline flood the bloodstream, heart rate increases, blood is redirected to large muscles, breathing becomes shallow, and the prefrontal cortex, which handles analytical thinking, long-term planning, and sound decisionmaking, is partially suppressed.

This response evolved for physical threats. For the vast majority of human history, dangers were immediate and required rapid physical response. The amygdala's speed and power were, in that context, adaptive. The complication is that the amygdala does not distinguish between a physical threat and a learned one. It responds to any stimulus that has been associated, through accumulated experience, with danger, pain, or loss.

For many people, financial stimuli have become exactly those learned threats. Not through a single dramatic event, necessarily, but through years of accumulated associations: the tension in a household where money was chronically tight, the argument overheard between parents about a bill, the atmosphere of a home that changed when something financial went wrong, the shame of an early adult debt, the anxiety of a monthly shortfall. These experiences are encoded at the level of implicit memory, they do not require conscious recall to activate. The amygdala simply pattern-matches incoming stimuli against its threat database and fires when it finds a match.

The practical consequence is the one that anyone who has felt their chest tighten when opening a credit card statement, or experienced a strong avoidance impulse when thinking about their retirement account, or found themselves unable to initiate the salary conversation despite weeks of preparation, will recognise immediately: the cognitive machinery most needed for good financial decisions is the machinery that financial anxiety most reliably degrades.

The Cognitive Cost of Financial Stress

The economists Sendhil Müllainathan and Eldar Shafir spent years studying what they called the bandwidth tax: the way that significant worry occupies cognitive resources that would otherwise be available for clear thinking. Their research, conducted with populations across different income levels and geographies, produced a finding that has direct implications for financial behaviour: people under significant financial stress performed measurably worse on cognitive tests, tests of fluid intelligence, decision quality, and impulse control, than the same people when their financial stress was lower.

The estimated cognitive degradation, across their studies, was equivalent to roughly thirteen IQ points. Not a permanent reduction. A state-dependent one, caused entirely by the cognitive load of financial worry occupying processing capacity that would otherwise be available for analytical thinking. Thirteen points. Consumed by background anxiety, unavailable for the financial reasoning that would reduce the anxiety.

The implication that matters most is the direction of causation. Financial stress does not just predict poor financial decisions. It causes them. The person who is most anxious about money is, in the moment of that anxiety, least neurologically equipped to make the financial decisions that would relieve it. The trap is both physiological and recursive, and it operates independently of income. A professional earning a substantial salary can be running this stress loop just as powerfully as someone earning much less, because the loop is driven by the ratio of anxiety to security, not by the absolute level of income.

During my time managing sales teams, first at ITC, later at Perfetti Van Melle, I watched this dynamic play out in the professional domain with uncomfortable regularity. The territory managers under the most personal financial pressure were consistently the ones who made their worst professional calls at the end of a difficult month, when commercial pressure was highest. They pushed channel inventory to hit a number that would create problems next quarter. They made concessions they did not have authority to make. They optimised for shortterm relief in ways that reliably created longer-term problems. The personal financial anxiety was bleeding into professional judgment, consuming resources that professional judgment required.

The Prefrontal Cortex: Your Wealth-Building Brain

The prefrontal cortex sits behind your forehead and is responsible for the cognitive functions most essential to building wealth over a lifetime: long-term planning, cost-benefit analysis, impulse control, the capacity to delay gratification, and the ability to hold competing possible futures in mind and evaluate them against each other.

It is also the brain region most sensitive to cortisol. When cortisol levels rise during the amygdala's threat response, prefrontal cortex activity measurably decreases. Its functions become less available precisely when they are most needed.

The moments of highest financial importance are therefore often the moments of lowest financial cognitive capacity. The person facing a sudden job loss, a market crash, a large unexpected expense, or a high-stakes salary conversation is simultaneously the person most in need of clear financial thinking and the person least biochemically equipped to produce it. Every financial pressure event generates its own cognitive tax that makes navigating the pressure harder than it would be under calm conditions.

The actionable implication is specific: if you can change the physiological state before engaging with financial decisions, reduce the cortisol, bring the prefrontal cortex back online, you will make consistently better financial decisions. This is not vague advice. There are specific, well-researched physiological techniques that accomplish this in under two minutes. We examine them in Chapter Six. For now, the important thing is the understanding: the solution to poor financial decisionmaking under stress is not more information or stronger resolve. It is regulation, changing the body's state before the decision is made.

What Buffett Actually Had That Others Didn't

Returning to 2008: what Buffett possessed that most investors lacked was not primarily superior knowledge, though he certainly had that. It was a trained, reliable capacity to access System Two under conditions of maximum emotional pressure.

This capacity is not innate. Buffett has described his own early investment experience as being accompanied by real anxiety. What changed over decades of deliberate practice was the construction of a framework stable enough to hold him when System One was generating maximum noise. The framework itself is famously simple: understand what you own, understand roughly what it is worth, buy it at a price that gives you a margin of safety, and hold it as long as the business remains sound. Simple enough to remember under duress. Specific enough to produce clear decisions in ambiguous situations. Empirically grounded enough to provide genuine confidence.

One of the practical goals of Part Three is to help you build equivalent anchors for your own financial life, frameworks simple enough to apply under stress, specific enough to produce guidance, and grounded in evidence rather than hope. Not for stock picking. For the foundational disciplines: regular investment, staying invested, addressing debt, capturing the compensation you have earned. Un-glamorous. Collectively, over the years of a working life, sufficient.

The Good News: The Brain Changes

Knowing your profile does not change the pattern. But it gives you the specific map you need to find the intervention points that will. That is where we go next.

In the next chapter, we move from the general neurological picture to the specific patterns through which that neurology expresses itself in individual financial lives. The four Wealth Profiles are the four most common ways that the brain's wealthblocking architecture manifests in practice: the four characteristic shapes that the same underlying mechanism takes when filtered through different individual histories and temperaments.

The neuroscience in this chapter provides the foundation for every practical tool in Part Three. Understanding that the problem is architectural rather than moral, that the avoidance and the anxiety and the poor decisions under stress are the outputs of a system doing what it was designed to do, in a context it was not designed for, is not an excuse. It is a diagnosis. And accurate diagnosis is the prerequisite for effective treatment.

Laying the Ground for What Comes Next

Everything in this chapter could, in the wrong reading, suggest a deterministic conclusion: the brain is wired this way, the patterns are entrenched, nothing can be done. This is precisely the wrong conclusion, and thirty years of neuroplasticity research contradicts it comprehensively.

Neuroplasticity: the brain's capacity to modify its own structure and function in response to new experience, is one of the most important scientific discoveries of the late twentieth century. The adult brain is not fixed. Neural pathways, which produce our habitual thoughts, emotional responses, and behavioural tendencies, are strengthened by repeated use and weakened by disuse. They can be replaced by new pathways built through new, repeated experience.

The threat associations built around financial engagement were created through accumulated experience. They are modified through a different kind of accumulated experience: the experience of engaging with financial material and discovering that the predicted catastrophe does not arrive. Each completed financial engagement is a small piece of counterevidence. Accumulated over weeks and months, that counterevidence updates the amygdala's prediction. The threat response becomes less intense. The threshold for triggering it rises. The space between stimulus and response, Frankl's space, grows.

This is slow. It is not linear. There is no single insight that rewires the response. What works is consistent practice: graduated, repeated engagement with financial material in a physiologically regulated state. The tools in Part Three are designed around this mechanism. They start smaller than might seem necessary precisely because the nervous system changes through experience, and experience must be tolerable to be educative.

The broader principle I want to establish here, and return to throughout the book: the solution to financial avoidance and poor decision-making under stress is not more information, stronger motivation, or greater willpower. It is regulation, changing the physiological state before the decision, so that the decision is made by the full version of your cognitive capacity rather than the cortisol-compromised version. Every practical tool in Part Three builds on this foundation.

We examine this technique in full practical detail in Chapter Six. I mention it here because the why matters as much as the how: cortisol suppresses the prefrontal cortex, the prefrontal cortex is your wealth-building brain, and regulated breathing reduces cortisol. That is the logical chain. The technique is not a trick. It is applied neuroscience.

I am not describing a mindfulness practice in any aspirational sense. I am describing a physiological intervention, a specific technique for changing the body's biochemical state before a cognitively demanding task. Surgeons use versions of it before operating. Military units use it before high-stakes field decisions. The mechanism is identical across all those contexts: reduce cortisol, restore prefrontal cortex function, make clear analytical thinking more accessible.

This forty-five-second sequence activates the parasympathetic nervous system and measurably reduces cortisol within about a minute. It brings the prefrontal cortex back online to a meaningful degree. The financial decision made from a partially regulated state is consistently better than the one made from a fully activated threat response.

Before any financial task, checking a balance, making a payment, thinking about a salary negotiation, pause for thirty seconds before beginning. Take three slow breaths with a longer exhale than inhale: four counts in, six counts out. Notice where in your body you are carrying tension. Name it, without trying to resolve it.

There is a practical implication of this chapter that I want to make explicit before we move on, because it is one of the most immediately useful things in this book.

The brain changes in response to what it does repeatedly. Change what you do, and the brain follows. That is the scientific basis for everything practical in this book.

1.3 Your Wealth Profile

Four patterns that determine how your money blocks show up — and which tools unlock them

"Know thyself"

- *Socrates*

About three years into my time at ITC, I noticed a pattern that the sales numbers alone could not explain.

I was managing a territory team, and the data showed clearly that some people consistently hit their numbers while others, despite similar market conditions and comparable skills, fell short in ways they struggled to account for. When I started paying closer attention to how the underperformers behaved under pressure. not the commercial pressure in the market but the personal financial pressure at home, what I saw was striking.

The salespeople who carried the most financial anxiety in their personal lives were the ones most likely to make poor decisions at the end of a difficult month. Under target pressure, they would push channel inventory to manufacture a number, knowing it would create problems the following month. They would offer terms they were not authorised to offer. They were solving today's anxiety in ways that reliably created tomorrow's problem.

This is well-documented in sales psychology: the way performance pressure degrades decision quality in predictable directions. What interested me was the personal dimension: the same anxiety pattern that showed up in their professional behaviour at month-end was also the pattern governing their personal financial lives. The two domains were not separate. They were the same pattern expressing itself in different arenas.

That observation eventually led me to what I now call Wealth Profiles: four characteristic ways that financial anxiety organizes itself in practice. Understanding yours is not an exercise in categorization. It is a diagnostic process that leads directly to the tools most likely to work for your particular pattern, because generic financial advice, designed for everyone, is optimized for no one.

Profile One: The Deferrer

The Deferrer's relationship with financial action is governed by a single, reliably recurring word: later.

Not never. Later. The Deferrer fully intends to act. They have researched the investment options. They may have downloaded the app. They know which fund they are going to use. They have had the internal conversation about why this matters and agreed with themselves that it does. The execution is the part that does not happen, pushed forward by the reliable discovery that now is not quite the right moment.

I know this profile clearly because I was a textbook version of it. The version of me that had three browser tabs open about index funds for four months without making a contribution was not uninformed or unmotivated. The mechanism was subtler than that: the moment of actual execution kept finding reasons to be not quite right. I would think: I should do this when I have more time to look into it properly. When I had more time, I would think: I should do this when I have chosen the specific fund. When I had chosen the fund, I would think: I should do this at the beginning of next month. The next month arrived. The cycle continued.

The discomfort driving this is not dramatic distress. It is the low-grade unease of entering unfamiliar territory, of committing to something irreversible in a domain where the outcomes are not fully within your control, of confronting, even briefly, the gap between where you are and where you intended to be. The discomfort is manageable. The Deferrer manages it in the most natural way available: by scheduling the confrontation for a future moment that is always almost here and never quite now.

The financial cost of the Deferrer pattern is the most invisible cost in personal finance, because it is defined entirely by what did not happen. There is no statement that shows foregone compounding. There is no charge labelled 'delay cost' on any account. The money that compound growth would have generated simply never existed, which makes it easy to not quite notice and difficult to feel the urgency of addressing.

The unlock for the Deferrer is structural rather than motivational. The Deferrer does not need more encouragement or more information. They need the execution decision removed from the loop entirely. Automation, setting up a recurring investment or savings transfer that happens on a fixed date without requiring a monthly decision, eliminates the recurring confrontation that triggers the deferral. When the action happens automatically, the discomfort of initiating it does not get to vote.

Profile Two: The Vigilance Trapper

The Vigilance Trapper appears, from the outside, to be the most financially engaged person in the room. They check their accounts multiple times a day. They follow market movements with the attention that other people give to sports scores. They have comprehensive, current knowledge of their financial position, or rather, of the short-term fluctuations in their financial position, which is a different thing.

The trap is that their engagement is organised entirely around threat detection rather than wealth creation. The dominant question is not 'what is the best move here?' It is 'what could go wrong, and am I protected?' Every market dip is a potential disaster. Every economic headline is personally relevant. The monitoring is constant and the anxiety it generates is constant, because short-term financial data is volatile by nature, and constant monitoring of volatile data produces constant emotional activation.

I worked for several years with a regional manager who was, professionally, one of the most decisive people I have encountered. In meetings, he moved quickly, committed clearly, and managed ambiguity with the easy confidence of someone who had handled worse. When I once, entirely by chance, had a conversation with him about his own investments, triggered by a volatile day in the markets, I watched the same man become someone else. Every sentence hedged into the next. Every potential action was immediately followed by the scenario in which it would go wrong. He was not afraid to act in his professional domain. When it came to his own money, he was frozen.

The Vigilance Trapper's financial cost is less visible than the Deferrer's but equally real. They hold too much in low-return cash positions because the market always feels uncertain. They exit investments at the first sign of volatility, locking in losses and missing recoveries. They spend enormous cognitive energy on monitoring that does not improve their position, and frequently worsens it, because frequent monitoring multiplies the opportunities for anxiety-driven decisions at exactly the wrong moments.

The fundamental investment discipline for a long-term investor is staying in. The Vigilance Trapper's entire psychological orientation works against this. Their monitoring transforms temporary price declines into emotionally intolerable events that must be responded to, precisely when the rational response is no response at all.

The unlock for the Vigilance Trapper is not more financial education, they typically have more than average already. It is planned inattention: a deliberate, in-advance decision about how frequently to look at long-term investments, agreed when calm and honoured when volatile. Quarterly reviews. The investment app moved off the home screen. Market news consumed weekly rather than constantly. The goal is not ignorance. It is recalibrating the time horizon of the monitoring to match the time horizon of the investment.

Profile Three: The Emotional Spender

The Emotional Spender has found, through accumulated experience, that purchasing provides reliable, immediate relief from whatever discomfort they are currently managing. This is not a failing of character. It is a learned connection between a feeling state and a behaviour that addresses it, and the connection was formed because it worked.

Cortisol, the primary stress hormone, increases the brain's sensitivity to dopamine, the neurotransmitter of reward and anticipation. Under stress, immediately available sources of dopamine become more compelling. In a consumer economy where almost anything can be purchased in seconds and delivered in hours, the pull toward spending under stress is biochemically amplified. Each purchase provides a genuine, if brief, dopamine hit. The relief is real. The mechanism is learned. The pattern is automatic.

The particularly insidious version of this pattern appears when the stress being managed is financial stress itself. The anxiety about not having built adequate savings drives the spending that prevents adequate savings from being built. The relief is temporary. The anxiety returns, slightly amplified by the spending that just occurred. The loop has no natural exit point.

Howard Schultz understood this mechanism intuitively when he built Starbucks. The company is not primarily in the business of selling coffee. It is in the business of providing a reliable, available, sensory hit of pleasure and comfort at the moment when a stressed urban professional most needs relief. The success of that business model is built on the same neurochemistry that drives the Emotional Spender's pattern. Recognising that does not make the pattern easier to change, but it does make it less shameful. The person who spends more than they intend to when they are stressed is not morally weak. They are using the most available tool for managing a real feeling. The work is not to eliminate the feeling or to condemn the tool. It is to develop better tools.

The unlock for the Emotional Spender begins before the spending decision, not at it. By the time the purchase is being contemplated, the biochemistry is already established and the urge is strong. The productive intervention point is earlier: developing the capacity to notice the emotional state that precedes the spending impulse, recognise it as stress rather than desire, and have alternative regulation strategies available before the spending channel activates. Chapter Six provides those strategies in practical detail.

Profile Four: The Control Architect

The Control Architect is, by most conventional measures, the most financially responsible of the four profiles. They have a budget. It is detailed and largely honoured. They track their spending with more precision than most people would find comfortable. They hit their savings targets. In the domain of financial discipline as it is conventionally defined, they have it.

What they often miss is the strategic picture: the larger financial landscape that their operational control system is optimising without stepping back to evaluate whether it is optimising the right things.

Jeff Bezos built Amazon on a principle he called regret minimisation: in any significant decision, ask which choice you will regret more at eighty, and decide accordingly. The framework was specifically designed to counteract the shortterm risk-aversion that rational analysis naturally produces when applied to genuinely uncertain situations. Without it, careful analysis will usually counsel caution. With it, the analysis is reoriented toward a longer time horizon where the cost of not acting often exceeds the cost of acting imperfectly.

The Control Architect needs a version of this reorientation. Not because the discipline is wrong, it produces real results in the domains it is applied to. But because the largest financial opportunities in a lifetime are almost never captured through meticulous optimisation of the known. They are captured through willingness to act on the uncertain: the salary negotiation whose outcome is not guaranteed, the investment strategy whose returns are not certain, the career move whose compensation implications require a conversation rather than a calculation. The Control Architect's system is well-calibrated for certainty and under-calibrated for ambiguity, and ambiguity is where the largest opportunities consistently live. One question that arises consistently live.

One question that arises consistently when I describe these profiles: what if I genuinely cannot identify which one I am? Uncertainty about your own pattern is itself useful information. It usually means one of two things. Either the pattern is operating so automatically that it has become invisible, it feels like your personality rather than a recognisable behaviour, or the pattern shifts depending on context, and you exhibit different profiles in different domains of your life.

Both are workable. For the pattern that has become invisible, the most reliable method is not introspection but observation. For the next two weeks, whenever you notice a financial task you intended to do and did not, write down what actually happened in the moment of not doing it. Not the rationalisation, what happened in real time. The physical sensation, the thought that arose, the thing you did instead. Two weeks of honest observation will surface the pattern more reliably than any amount of retrospective analysis.

For the genuinely split pattern, the question is what triggers the switch. Most people who exhibit different financial profiles in different contexts find that the switch is driven by a specific variable: solo versus shared decision-making, professional versus personal domain, high-stakes versus low-stakes amounts, calm versus stressed emotional baseline. Identifying the trigger identifies the context where the costliest pattern is operating, which is exactly the context that most needs the specific tools designed for it.

There is one dimension of the profile conversation I want to address directly before we move on: the relationship between financial profile and identity. Many people, on recognising themselves in one of these patterns, interpret the recognition as confirmation of a fixed truth. I am a Deferrer. I am not someone who can handle money. This is just how I am.

This interpretation is understandable and incorrect. The profiles describe behavioural patterns, not identity. A pattern is something that happens repeatedly and automatically in response to specific stimuli. It was formed through accumulated experience and is maintained through repetition. Both of those facts mean it is changeable, through the same mechanism that formed it: accumulated new experience, this time pointing in a different direction.

The Deferrer who automates a monthly investment and lets it run for six months has six months of evidence that financial action does not require a monthly decision crisis. The Vigilance Trapper who holds through a volatile quarter has evidence that not-checking was survivable. The Emotional Spender who uses the breathing technique from Chapter Six and does not spend has evidence that stress can be managed without a purchase. Each piece of evidence is small. Together, over weeks and months, they change the pattern. That is how it works. That is how it has always worked.

In my own financial life, I recognise traces of this profile clearly. I was meticulous about certain habits and completely unstrategic about others. not from inattention but because the discipline had become self-referential: consistent about the things it had decided to be consistent about, resistant to evaluating whether those were the right things. The grocery spending was optimised. The salary had not been formally negotiated in two years. I was managing the trees with precision and not looking at the forest.

The unlock for the Control Architect is not more discipline, they have that. It is a deliberate, calendar-marked practice of stepping back from the operational system at least once a year to evaluate the system itself: whether it is optimising the most important variables, whether the risks it avoids are accurately calibrated, whether the larger trajectory is being seen clearly or obscured by the comfortable detail.

Reading Your Profile and What It Tells You

Most people who read through these four profiles will find one that lands with a recognisable specificity the others do not. Many will find a clear primary with traces of a secondary, the Vigilance Trapper with Deferrer tendencies in certain domains, the Emotional Spender with Control Architect habits in certain categories. A small number will feel genuinely split between two, which usually means the pattern shifts by context: rigorous at work, avoidant at home, or precise about spending and paralysed about investing.

All of these combinations are workable. The profile is not a diagnosis. It is a current pattern, specific enough to be described, and therefore specific enough to be changed. The Deferrer can learn to act. The Vigilance Trapper can learn to hold. The Emotional Spender can develop better regulation tools. The Control Architect can learn to look up from the system. These are behavioural adjustments, not personality transformations.

Throughout the practical chapters that follow, I will indicate which tools are most directly relevant to which profile. But before moving forward, there is one question worth sitting with now: what has your pattern cost you, in specific terms, over the last three years? Not as an exercise in regret. As the beginning of a clear-eyed calculation about what is still available, and why the work of addressing it is worth doing.

In the next chapter, we put numbers to what your profile has been costing you. The Opportunity Audit in Chapter Four is the most important practical exercise in this book. It converts the abstract understanding of Part One into a specific, personal figure, your figure, your opportunity, your starting line. Do it honestly. The number it produces is not a verdict. It is a map. And maps, for the first time, make navigation possible.

What does not tend to shift automatically, without specific intervention, is the pattern that is currently most active. That pattern will continue to cost what it costs until something changes the conditions that are maintaining it. The purpose of the profile framework is to make that pattern visible enough to name, specific enough to address, and mapped to the interventions that are most likely to work.

One thing I have noticed consistently in watching professionals engage with this framework: the profile that costs you most today is not necessarily the profile that has been most operative throughout your financial life. Profiles shift. A professional who was a Deferrer in their twenties may develop Control Architect tendencies as their income and responsibilities grow. Someone who was an Emotional Spender during a period of high professional stress may find that pattern receding as the stress reduces, replaced by a more benign form of the Vigilance Trapper as their financial awareness increases.

A Final Observation on Profiles and Time

The next chapter puts numbers to that calculation.

This is the principle that runs through the entire practical section of this book. Not overcoming patterns through force of will. Changing the conditions so that the pattern has less purchase, the better action has less resistance, and the compound effect of consistent good decisions can begin to do its work.

In each case, the intervention works not because it overrides the pattern with willpower but because it changes the conditions under which the pattern operates. Automation does not require the Deferrer to feel more motivated. It simply removes the decision point. The scheduled review does not require the Vigilance Trapper to feel less anxious. It simply structures when the anxiety is engaged with and when it is not. The breathing practice does not require the Emotional Spender to want to spend less. It changes the physiological state that the spending was attempting to regulate.

For the Deferrer, automation removes the monthly execution decision and with it the monthly activation of the avoidance pattern. For the Vigilance Trapper, a scheduled quarterly review with a written policy about what conditions would trigger a change removes the daily emotional exposure to short-term volatility. For the Emotional Spender, the physiological regulation practice intercepts the stress-spending loop at the point where it can actually be interrupted. For the Control Architect, the annual strategic review creates a sanctioned context for the big-picture thinking the operational system has been crowding out.

This is why the prescription must match the profile. Generic financial advice tells you to start investing, negotiate your salary, and pay down debt. Those priorities are correct as a set of intentions and useless as instructions for the person who already knows them and cannot reliably execute them.

The instruction that actually helps is the one that addresses the specific mechanism blocking the specific action.

Understanding why the profiles matter requires understanding one thing clearly: the same financial action produces different psychological costs for different profiles. A five-hundred-dollar monthly investment contribution is a trivial decision for someone who does not have the Deferrer pattern in this domain, requiring no particular effort or attention. For someone who does, it is a monthly confrontation with a threat response that has been running for years. The action is identical. The psychological cost is completely different.

The Connection Between Profile and Practice

Read it in order the first time. The chapter that follows makes the case for what is at stake. Part Two shows you why the gap exists. Part Three gives you the specific tools to close it. Part Four shows you how to hold what you have built. Let us begin.

1.4 The Opportunity Audit

Counting what is available to you, and what it costs to keep waiting

"Clarity is the most important thing. I can compare clarity to pruning in gardening: without it, nothing works"

- *Diane von Furstenberg*

A particular kind of financial discomfort exists that is different from the ordinary anxiety of money. It is the discomfort of knowing, without quite knowing.

You know, roughly, that you should be investing more than you are. You know, roughly, that your salary may be below what the market would pay for someone with your experience. You know, at some level, that the credit card balance is costing you more than it appears to. But the figures are vague. The calculations have never been done. And vagueness, as it turns out, is one of the most reliable protections against the urgency that would otherwise demand action.

This chapter removes the vagueness. Its sole purpose is to produce a number: your number, calculated honestly from your specific income, your specific position, and your patterns. Not a number designed to be inspiring. Not a hypothetical projection built on best-case assumptions. The real, calculable cost of your current financial behaviour, and the real, still-available opportunity that remains.

The exercise is called the Opportunity Audit, and it takes thirty to forty-five minutes done carefully, fifteen done quickly. The honest version is worth more than the careful one. A rough honest number, held clearly, produces more useful urgency than a precise number softened by optimistic inputs.

Before we begin, I want to establish something clearly about what this exercise is not. It is not an audit of your failures. It is not designed to make you feel behind, inadequate, or guilty. Those feelings may arise briefly, because honest financial selfassessment sometimes produces them, and that is worth acknowledging rather than pretending otherwise. But they are not the goal. The goal is clarity. And clarity, unlike shame, points forward.

Why You Need a Number, Not a Principle

Personal finance is full of principles. Invest regularly. Compound interest is the eighth wonder of the world. Negotiate your salary. Pay off expensive debt aggressively. Every one of these principles is true. None of them, in my observation, has ever motivated a single financial action in the absence of a personal number attached to it.

Principles are abstract. Numbers are specific. Specificity creates urgency that abstraction cannot.

When I finally ran the calculation on my own compounding delay cost, sitting with a financial calculator one evening after a long week at Kenvue, the figure that appeared was not what I expected. I had told myself, in the comfortable fog of good intentions, that the gap was manageable. That a few years of inconsistency would be recovered easily. The actual number, calculated from my age, my investment horizon, and the difference in starting dates, said something different. It said: this is real, it is large, and every additional month of delay adds to it in a specific and calculable way.

That number changed how I behaved. Not through shame, but through the replacement of comfortable vagueness with uncomfortable specificity. I could no longer not know. And not knowing, it turned out, had been doing a great deal of work in maintaining my inaction.

Your version of that number is waiting in this chapter. The audit has four sections, and each produces one figure. Add them together at the end and you have your personal opportunity number: the financial gap between where you are and where your income and time horizon say you could be.

Section One: The Compounding Opportunity

In 1984, a twenty-three-year-old woman named Sylvia started her first professional job. Her friend Catherine, the same age, started hers the same month. Both earned similar salaries. Both had the same general awareness that investing was something responsible adults did.

Sylvia started putting away a modest amount every month from her first paycheck. Nothing dramatic. She automated it so she never had to decide again. Catherine kept meaning to start when things were a bit more settled.

By the time both women were sixty-five, Sylvia's account had grown into something that gave her options Catherine did not have. Not because Sylvia was better with money in any sophisticated sense. She was not a skilled investor. She chose simple, boring, diversified funds and left them alone. What Sylvia had that Catherine did not was the forty-two years of compound growth on every contribution, rather than the thirtytwo years Catherine eventually accumulated when she finally started ten years later.

The difference between their outcomes was not talent, not knowledge, not discipline in any heroic sense. It was ten years. Which is to say, it was time. Which is to say, it was starting when you know you should rather than when the conditions feel right.

For your version of this calculation, you need three honest inputs.

First: your current age and the age at which you plan to substantially reduce your working income. The gap between those two numbers is your investment horizon in years.

Second: the monthly amount you could realistically invest right now, without genuine hardship. Not the aspirationally comfortable version that sounds good when you imagine it. The number that would actually leave your essential expenses covered and a small buffer intact. If that number is lower than you would like, that is fine. Starting small is not a compromise.

It is, as Chapter Eleven explains in detail, actually the correct strategy for how the brain changes.

Third: a return assumption. Historical long-run average annual returns for a diversified equity index in most developed markets have been in the range of seven to ten percent in real terms. Eight percent is a reasonable and defensible planning assumption, conservative enough to survive most historical market environments.

Use any compound interest calculator, freely available online in any currency, and calculate what that monthly investment produces at eight percent over your investment horizon.

Then ask one more question: how long ago did you first tell yourself you were going to start investing consistently? If the honest answer is two years, add two years to the horizon and recalculate. The difference between the two figures is your compounding delay cost. That is the money your delay has already cost you, expressed as a specific number rather than a principle.

For most mid-career professionals, this figure is larger than they expected before calculating it. I have sat with enough people through this exercise to know that the first reaction is usually a quiet moment of recognition: this is real, and it is larger than the comfortable fog allowed me to believe. That recognition is not a reason for despair. The past is fixed. The horizon from today forward is not. Every year of consistent investment that begins now produces returns that compound forward on exactly the same maths.

The Warren Buffett Illustration

Warren Buffett made approximately ninety-five percent of his net worth after the age of sixty-five. This fact is cited often, usually to make a point about patience in investing. The deeper point is about the arithmetic of compound growth over very long time horizons.

Buffett did not become meaningfully better at investing in his late sixties. His methods were essentially consistent from early adulthood. What changed was the mathematics: the curve of compound growth, which is gradual in the early decades and then becomes genuinely dramatic in the later ones, had finally reached its steep phase. The same investment behaviour that had produced solid but unremarkable results for thirty years began, in the fourth and fifth decades, to produce extraordinary ones.

Most investors do not have Buffett's time horizon. But every investor has more of it than they are typically using. The professional who starts investing consistently at thirty-two instead of twenty-eight has shortened their steep-curve phase by four years. Those four years, in the context of a total sixty-year possible investment horizon, do not sound large. The numbers say otherwise.

The Compounding Opportunity figure you just calculated is your version of this illustration, made personal. Write it down. Keep it somewhere you will see it at the beginning of every month for the next three months. Not as a source of guilt. As a standing reminder of what the month you are entering is worth, financially, if you use it well.

Section Two: The Compensation Opportunity

Of all the financial opportunities most professionals leave unclaimed, the salary gap is the one that produces the most consistently surprised reactions when it is properly calculated. Because the gap itself is almost always larger than people estimate, and because its ten-year impact, once the compounding effect on future raises is included, is substantially larger still.

Linda Babcock and Sara Laschever, whose research on negotiation has been influential in both academic and professional contexts, documented a finding that has held up across subsequent studies: professionals who negotiate their starting salary and negotiate consistently at performance reviews earn significantly more over their careers than those who accept what is offered. The mechanism is multiplicative. Each successful negotiation raises the base from which the next raise is calculated. Each job change is benchmarked against the current figure. A salary that has been consistently at the lower end of the market range compounds downward through every subsequent step.

For your audit, the process has three steps.

Research your current market rate using at least three independent sources. Job listing databases, professional network salary tools, and a brief conversation with a recruiter who works in your specific sector will typically produce a reliable range. Find the median and the 75th percentile for your role, your years of experience, and your city or region. Be honest about what your profile is. This is not the moment for aspirational benchmarking.

Compare those figures to your current compensation. If you are below the median, you have a confirmed compensation gap. Write down the annual figure: what the median pays minus what you currently earn. If you are at the median, there is a legitimate evidenced case for moving toward the 75th percentile based on specific contributions and performance, and the gap between those two points is your opportunity figure.

Multiply the annual gap by ten. The ten-year figure is the right one to use because it captures the compounding effect of a higher base on every future raise and job offer. A salary improvement of ten thousand per year is not just ten thousand per year. It is a higher starting point for every percentage increase you receive for the rest of your time in the workforce. The ten-year total, for most mid-career professionals with a confirmed gap, is a number that produces a particular quality of quiet determination.

The Conversation That Most People Avoid

Something honest about why the compensation gap persists for so many intelligent professionals for so many intelligent, performing professionals, because understanding the why is the first step to changing it.

In my years managing teams at Perfetti Van Melle and later at Kenvue, I observed a consistent pattern in how high performers related to their own compensation. Commercially, many of them were confident negotiators. They understood margin, they understood value, they understood how to make a case for a price. Applied to their own salary, that same capability went largely quiet.

The difference is not one of skill. It is one of emotional valence. Commercial negotiations are external: you are representing the organisation's interests in a context where the relationship stakes are operational. A salary negotiation is internal: you are asserting a claim about your own worth in a context where the relationship is personal and the potential rejection feels like a judgement about you rather than about a price. The discomfort is not irrational. It is a very understandable response to a genuinely vulnerable situation.

But it has a cost. And that cost, calculated accurately, is almost always large enough to make the discomfort worth managing rather than avoiding. Chapter Fourteen provides the full preparation framework for the compensation conversation: how to research, how to document your contributions specifically, how to make the ask in a way that is professional rather than confrontational, and how to respond productively regardless of what comes back. For now, write the figure in your audit and let it be what it is.

Section Three: The Structural Efficiency Opportunity

This section of the audit is the most variable across different countries and tax environments, and I have deliberately left it general for that reason. What is universal is the principle: most tax codes in most countries contain provisions specifically designed to encourage long-term saving and retirement investment, and most earning professionals do not fully utilise them.

The reasons are not typically ignorance. Most professionals are vaguely aware that provisions exist. The reason is engagement cost: actually navigating the details of available deductions, employer matching arrangements, tax-advantaged account structures, and salary restructuring options produces enough friction and discomfort to be perpetually deferred. The result is that money that could have been kept is given away every year, quietly and without a specific line item to make it visible.

One meeting with a qualified tax professional asking one specific question changes this: given my current income, my employer arrangement, and my financial structure, what provisions am I not currently utilising, and what would it take to change that? One meeting, held once, produces an annual benefit that recurs every year thereafter. The cost of the meeting is typically recovered within weeks of implementing the recommendations.

If you have already had this conversation and know your specific figure, use it. If you have not, write a placeholder in your audit: structural efficiency opportunity to be confirmed with professional advice. The act of writing it there means it exists as a named item in your financial picture rather than a vague awareness that something might be possible. Named items get addressed. Vague awarenesses do not.

Section Four: The Debt Drag Opportunity

List every debt you currently carry. For each one, write the outstanding balance and the annual interest rate. Multiply balance by rate to get the annual interest cost. Add all the annual interest costs together.

This total is the amount you are paying each year to service existing debt: money that is not building your net worth, not funding experiences you value, not going anywhere except to the lender's profit line. It is the annual cost of carrying the debt at its current pace rather than addressing it more aggressively.

For context: the guaranteed return on eliminating debt at twenty-two percent interest is twenty-two percent. There is no widely available investment that offers a guaranteed twenty-two percent return. For anyone carrying consumer debt at high interest rates, aggressive debt clearance is not just a financial priority. It is the highest-return financial action currently available to them, on a guaranteed basis, with no market risk attached.

Write the total annual debt service cost in your audit. This is the amount that becomes available for wealth-building when the debt is cleared. It does not become available all at once, obviously. But the trajectory of aggressive clearance versus minimum payment is dramatically different over a three-to-fiveyear horizon, and the difference between those two trajectories is entirely within your control.

Reading Your Total

Add the four figures: the compounding opportunity, the compensation opportunity, the structural efficiency opportunity, and the debt drag opportunity. The result is your personal opportunity number.

Most professionals who complete this honestly find a total that is meaningfully larger than their intuitive estimate. This is expected and not accidental. All four components are largely invisible in normal financial life because they are defined by absence: what did not grow, what was not earned, what was not kept, what was not freed up. The audit makes the absences visible. And visible gaps are actionable in a way that invisible ones are not.

There is one additional calculation worth doing. Take your compounding opportunity and calculate the specific cost of one more year of delay: the difference between starting today and starting twelve months from now. For most people in the middle of their working lives, this figure, expressed as a specific monthly or annual number, is the most useful single output of the entire exercise. It converts the abstract importance of starting into the concrete cost of not starting, measured in units of actual money rather than units of principle.

Your number will tell you something too. Let it.

Ronald Read, the janitor whose story opened this book, did not have a complex investment strategy. What he had was the specific, consistent clarity about what he was building and why. His clarity was not dramatic or self-conscious.

It expressed itself in the quiet automation of a behaviour he maintained for six decades. But at some point, he must have done a version of the calculation that this chapter describes. He must have seen the number. And the number must have told him something specific enough to build a practice around.

The feeling that followed was not shame, though shame was briefly present. It was closer to relief. The specific relief of having looked at something honestly rather than maintaining the careful peripheral avoidance that keeps things vague. Vagueness requires energy to sustain. Clarity, even uncomfortable clarity, is less exhausting than the ongoing effort of not quite looking.

When I finally sat down and did it, on a Sunday afternoon with my phone off, the compounding delay figure was larger than I had allowed myself to imagine.

Not catastrophic, but specific enough that the comfortable fog of vague intention dissolved completely. I could no longer not know. And not knowing, I realised in that moment, had been doing a great deal of work in maintaining the comfortable situation of meaning to act without actually acting.

I had been in a period of heavy commercial travel, the kind where you spend more nights in hotel rooms than in your own bed and where anything requiring sustained attention beyond the immediate quarter tends to get mentally filed as something to address when the pace changes. The pace rarely changes at the speed you expect it to, and I had been filing the Opportunity Audit under that category for several months.

I want to describe what happened the first time I did this exercise honestly, because the experience is more common than people admit, and knowing it in advance makes it easier to sit with.

The Moment When the Number Becomes Real

Write that figure somewhere you will see it regularly. Not to produce guilt, which is not a sustainable motivator, but to maintain the specificity that vagueness erodes.

The opportunity audit is not a one-time exercise. Repeat it annually, on the same date each year, as part of the Annual Strategic Review in Chapter Twelve.

Watch the figures change as you act on them. The trajectory of that change, over three or four years of honest engagement, is one of the most motivating documents you will ever produce about your own financial life.

Write the total. Look at it once a day for the next week. Not to feel bad about the past, which is fixed. To feel the specific urgency of the future, which is not. Part Two explains precisely what has been creating that gap. Part Three closes it.

Part 2

UNDERSTAND YOUR PATTERNS

The internal architecture of what has been blocking your wealth

2.1 The Loop That Locks Wealth Out

How avoidance patterns are built, why they persist, and where they can be broken

'Nothing in life is to be feared. It is only to be understood. Now is the time to understand more, so that we may fear less"

- *Marie Curie*

In 2003, a behavioural economist named Shlomo Benartzi ran an experiment that would become one of the most replicated findings in the field.

He was working with companies trying to increase employee participation in retirement savings programmes. The standard approach, then as now, was education: explain the importance of saving, show the compound interest projections, make the case. Companies had been doing this for years with modest results. Benartzi tried something different. Instead of trying to persuade employees to save more now, he asked them to commit to saving more in the future, specifically out of their next salary increase. They would not feel the reduction today. The sacrifice was real but deferred.

Participation rates roughly tripled.

The finding illuminated something important about how financial behaviour actually works. The employees who declined to increase their current savings contribution were not irrational or unmotivated. They were experiencing a very specific and predictable resistance to present sacrifice for future benefit. That resistance, in the context of consistent financial habits, has a name and a mechanism. Understanding both is more useful than any amount of motivational encouragement.

The mechanism is the Wealth Lock Loop. It is not unique to retirement savings. It governs the avoidance of salary negotiations, the delay in starting investments, the minimal debt payment, the unreviewed insurance policy. It is the single most common internal obstacle to financial progress that I have observed across my career and in my own financial life. And it is addressable, precisely because it has a structure.

The Five Stages, Described Precisely

Most descriptions of avoidance are too general to be useful. This one is specific, because specificity is what allows you to recognise the loop while it is running rather than only in retrospect.

The loop begins with what I call a wealth trigger. Something introduces financial awareness into your experience. A notification from your bank. A colleague's mention of their investment portfolio. A birthday that makes you calculate how far from retirement you are. A moment of reading about markets. The trigger does not need to be large or dramatic. For a nervous system that has learned to associate financial engagement with discomfort, the trigger can be very small and still initiate the full sequence.

The trigger activates the second stage: the block response. This is the amygdala's threat signal arriving before conscious thought has formed. Cortisol enters the bloodstream. The thinking narrows and becomes circular rather than productive. A familiar internal conversation begins: I should deal with this. I will deal with this. Not right now, the timing is not quite right. This weekend. Next month. When things settle down. The rationalisation is different for different people but the quality is always the same: plausible, individually reasonable, and reliably preventing action.

The third stage is disengagement. To relieve the discomfort of the second stage, attention moves away from the trigger. The banking app is closed. The browser tab is switched. The thought is redirected toward something more immediately manageable. The relief that follows is immediate and genuine. The cortisol drops. The nervous system settles. In that moment, the disengagement has worked.

That genuine relief is the fourth stage, and it is the most important one for understanding why the loop persists. The brain has recorded a lesson: disengagement produces relief. This lesson is not recorded consciously or deliberately. It is recorded at the level of automatic learning, below the threshold of deliberate thought. But the recording is real and it will be applied again, with greater automaticity, the next time a similar trigger appears.

The fifth stage is the return of the trigger, now slightly amplified. More time has passed. The opportunity is slightly more urgent. The awareness that you deferred it again is itself an additional weight that makes the next trigger slightly more potent. The loop has completed one cycle. It will run the next one with somewhat less friction, because avoidance has been practised once more.

Repeated across months and years, this sequence does not stay constant. It intensifies. Triggers become more potent. The block response becomes more automatic. The disengagement becomes more reflexive. What began as a mild hesitation around financial engagement becomes a well-worn neural pathway that activates before the thought has fully formed. The avoidance, at that stage, does not feel like avoidance. It feels like reality: I am simply not a financial person, I have never been good with money, this is just how I am.

It is not how you are. It is how the loop has trained you to be. The distinction matters enormously, because patterns can be changed and identities feel permanent.

Why Trying Harder Is the Wrong Response

The conventional prescription for avoidance is willpower: push through the discomfort, make yourself do the thing, overcome the resistance with effort and determination. This prescription is not merely ineffective. It is counterproductive in a specific and predictable way.

Willpower is a prefrontal cortex function. It is the deliberate override of an impulse through conscious analytical effort. In conditions where the prefrontal cortex is fully online and operating at capacity, willpower works reasonably well for managing impulses.

The complication is that the second stage of the Wealth Lock Loop, the block response, has already partially disabled the prefrontal cortex through the cortisol release of the amygdala's threat signal. By the time you are trying to apply willpower to override the avoidance impulse, the system that produces willpower has already been compromised by the system that produces avoidance. You are trying to use a tool that has been partially disabled against the mechanism that disabled it.

This is why the experience of willpower-based financial resolutions is so consistent across so many different people: intense and genuine in the moment of making them, significantly less available one or two weeks later when the conditions that produced the resolution have passed and the normal patterns have reasserted themselves. The resolution was real. The mechanism producing the avoidance was not addressed by the resolution. The avoidance returns.

The loop must be interrupted at a different stage. Not at the disengagement moment, where willpower attempts to intervene and finds itself compromised. At the block response stage, before the cortisol has fully established the cognitive environment that makes disengagement automatic. The tools for interrupting stage two are physiological rather than cognitive. We examine them in detail in Chapter Six.

The Shame Amplifier

There is one element of the Wealth Lock Loop that makes it significantly more durable and significantly more resistant to change, and I want to address it directly because avoiding it is a form of the avoidance this chapter is about.

Shame.

Shame operates differently from guilt in a way that has direct practical implications. Guilt says: I did something that falls short of my values. That statement is about a behaviour, and behaviours can be changed. Shame says: I am someone who falls short. That statement is about an identity, and identities feel fixed. The person experiencing guilt looks for a different behaviour. The person experiencing shame looks for ways to avoid the evidence of their failing, because changing an identity feels overwhelming in a way that changing a behaviour does not.

When financial avoidance is accompanied by shame, and it very frequently is, the Wealth Lock Loop gains a reinforcing layer that makes each cycle more entrenched than the last. Each avoided financial task becomes additional evidence for the shameful identity. Each piece of evidence makes the identity feel more fixed. Each step toward financial engagement feels like walking into a courtroom where the verdict is already known.

Brene Brown's research on shame and vulnerability has established something practically important for anyone trying to change financial behaviour: shame is not an effective driver of sustained behavioural change. It drives short, reactive bursts of action, the frantic late-night budget session that produces a resolution and is abandoned within a fortnight, and then longer periods of numbing and avoidance. What drives sustained change is the thing shame prevents: honest, compassionate engagement with the pattern as a pattern rather than as a character verdict.

The frame that makes this possible is simple and not easy to hold: the avoidance you have been experiencing is not evidence of your character. It is the output of a specific neural loop that was built through accumulated experience and that runs automatically because that is what learned patterns do. You did not choose the experiences that built it. You are not obligated to continue being governed by it. Understanding this clearly, without either self-condemnation or self-congratulation, is the psychological foundation from which genuine change becomes possible.

Throughout this book, I try to hold that frame consistently. The patterns are described with precision because precision is what makes them changeable. They are not described with judgment because judgment produces shame and shame produces more avoidance. The goal is clarity, not verdict.

Three Points Where the Loop Can Be Broken

The Wealth Lock Loop can be interrupted at three distinct points. They operate at different timescales, require different kinds of effort, and produce different kinds of benefit. Understanding all three is important because different profiles, different situations, and different stages of the change process will make different entry points most accessible.

The first entry point is before the trigger arrives. This is the prevention strategy, and it is the most powerful because it removes the need to navigate the loop at all. Automation accomplishes this for recurring financial decisions: the investment contribution that transfers automatically on the 5th of every month does not require a monthly decision, does not generate a monthly trigger, and does not run the loop. The Deferrer who automates their investment has not overcome their Deferrer pattern. They have built a system that bypasses it. The distinction matters because bypassing is more durable than overcoming.

The second entry point is at stage two, the block response, before the cortisol surge has fully compromised prefrontal cortex function. Physiological regulation techniques, specifically the controlled breathing practice described in Chapter Six, can restore enough prefrontal cortex capacity within forty-five seconds to make the subsequent engagement possible from a more functional baseline. This entry point requires practice to use effectively, because it must be applied at the right moment and with sufficient consistency to become automatic. But once it is, it changes the experience of financial engagement at the level where the block is actually generated.

The third entry point is gradual evidence accumulation over time. Every time you engage with financial material and the predicted catastrophe does not follow, you deposit a small piece of counter-evidence into the amygdala's threat-prediction database. Accumulated over weeks and months, that counterevidence changes the prediction itself. The trigger that once generated a strong block response begins to generate a weaker one. The threshold for the avoidance response rises. The loop loosens.

This third entry point is the slowest and the most durable. It is also the one that operates as the natural output of every other practice in Part Three: the weekly financial review, the automated contributions, the debt clearance progress, the salary conversation completed. Each of these is simultaneously a financial action and a piece of evidence. The financial and the psychological benefits compound together.

Recognising the Loop in Real Time

One of the most practically useful skills in financial behaviour change is the ability to recognise the Wealth Lock Loop while it is actually running, rather than only in retrospect. This sounds simple and is surprisingly difficult, because the loop is self-concealing: the rationalisations it generates in stage two feel genuinely reasonable while they are being generated.

The most reliable indicator that the loop is running is not the content of the rationalisation but its timing. If the rationalisation arrives immediately after a financial trigger, within seconds, before you have had time to actually evaluate the situation, you are probably in stage two of the loop. Genuine reasons for deferring a financial action exist. They take longer to form than the loop's automatic response. Immediacy is the tell.

The second indicator is the presence of a physical sensation in the body: the chest tightening, the shallow breathing, the particular quality of cognitive narrowing that accompanies the cortisol response. These physical signals are the block response expressing itself in the body before the mind has constructed the rationalisation. Learning to notice them is the subject of the next chapter. For now, the important thing is to know they exist and that they are information rather than noise.

The third indicator is the pattern over time. If you find yourself regularly intending to take a specific financial action and regularly not taking it, and if the reasons for not taking it always sound plausible but always result in the same outcome, you are observing a loop rather than a series of independent reasonable decisions. The loop's signature is consistency: the same trigger, the same response, the same outcome, across many cycles.

Recognising these three indicators in real time creates what Viktor Frankl described as the space between stimulus and response. That space, however brief, is where choice becomes possible. It is not a large space, especially in the early stages of building this awareness. It is enough.

The loop does not define you. It describes a pattern that was built through experience. And patterns built through experience are changed through experience. That is the only mechanism that has ever worked.

Knowing your profile tells you what your loop looks like. The five stages are the same. The entry points most accessible to you depend on which profile you are working with, and the chapters in Part Three flag this explicitly where it is relevant.

For the Control Architect, the loop is most subtly embedded. The meticulous operational system is, in part, a sophisticated avoidance structure: by filling the available financial attention with the management of well-defined operational variables, it creates a legitimate reason not to engage with the larger strategic questions where the threat response is strongest. The loop hides inside genuine competence, which makes it the most difficult of the four to recognise from inside it.

For the Emotional Spender, the loop is the most behaviourally visible: trigger arrives, block response generates discomfort, disengagement takes the form of a purchase rather than a simple withdrawal of attention. The spending relieves the cortisol in the same way that closing the banking app does. The financial consequences are more immediately tangible, which is one of the reasons this profile often comes to attention sooner than the others.

For the Vigilance Trapper, the loop runs in reverse, in a sense. The trigger is not avoided; it is engaged with obsessively. But the engagement is organised around threat detection rather than wealth building, and the compulsive monitoring is itself a form of the avoidance response: it provides a feeling of doing something while preventing the calmer, longer-horizon engagement that would actually serve the financial position. The loop hides inside the appearance of diligence.

For the Deferrer, the loop runs quietly and almost invisibly. There is no dramatic avoidance, no obvious anxiety. Just the reliable production of a slightly-not-right moment that perpetually prevents execution. The Deferrer experiences the loop as a mild forward pressure, always toward a future moment that is marginally better prepared for action than the current one.

One thing that consistently surprises people when they first hear about the Wealth Lock Loop is how differently it manifests across the four Wealth Profiles described in Chapter Three. The loop is the same mechanism in all four cases. Its symptoms look almost nothing alike.

The Loop Across Different Profiles

What Breaking the Loop Actually Looks Like

Here is an honest description of what breaking the Wealth Lock Loop looks like in practice, because the description matters for what you expect from the process in Part Three.

Breaking the loop does not look like a transformation. It does not look like the moment you finally decide to take your finances seriously and everything clicks into place and the resistance disappears. That moment does not exist. If you are waiting for it, you will be waiting a long time, and the waiting will feel reasonable at every stage because the loop will provide plausible reasons for it.

Breaking the loop looks like this: a financial trigger arrives. The block response begins, the familiar tightening, the familiar impulse to close and redirect. And this time, you pause for thirty seconds. You take three slow breaths. You open one account. You look at one balance. You close the app. You write one sentence in a notebook.

Nothing catastrophic happens.

That is the break. Not a triumph. A small, specific, evidenced contradiction of the loop's prediction. The amygdala predicted: engage with this and something bad will follow. You engaged, on a very limited scale, and nothing bad followed. The prediction has been updated by one data point. Repeat this, consistently, over weeks and months, and the prediction changes. The trigger becomes less potent. The block response becomes less automatic. The loop, which once felt like an immovable feature of your relationship with money, begins to loosen.

That loosening is what the practices in Part Three are designed to produce. Not willpower. Not resolution. Accumulated, tolerable, specific counter-evidence, until the financial engagement that once activated a threat response begins to feel, if not comfortable, then at least ordinary.

Ordinary is enough. Ordinary sustained over years is what builds wealth.

The loop is neurological. The intervention is physiological. Chapter Six introduces the body-level practice that makes the loop breakable in real time, in the moment the trigger arrives, before the avoidance has fully engaged.

2.2 Your Body Knows Where the Money Is

The physical dimension of financial anxiety, and the most direct way to address it

"The body is the unconscious mind. Repressed emotions find expression in the body"

- *Candace Pert*

In 2011, the neuroscientist Antonio Damasio documented something that should have been more disruptive to conventional financial thinking than it was.

Damasio had been studying patients who had suffered damage to the orbitofrontal cortex, the region of the brain that integrates emotional signals with rational analysis. These patients retained their full intellectual and analytical capabilities. They could reason clearly, perform complex calculations, understand probabilities, and evaluate options against each other. What they could not do, reliably, was make decisions.

Without the emotional input that the orbitofrontal cortex normally processes, their analytical systems could generate options but could not choose between them. They would deliberate for hours over decisions that typical people resolve in seconds. Not because they were less intelligent. Because decision-making, it turned out, requires feeling as well as thinking. Emotion is not the enemy of good judgment. It is a necessary component of it.

This finding matters for our purposes because it reframes what we are trying to do when we talk about managing financial anxiety. The goal is not to eliminate emotional processing from financial decisions, which Damasio showed is both impossible and counterproductive. The goal is to regulate the emotional processing so that it operates at the right intensity. Not the overwhelming intensity of a full threat response, which shuts down analytical capacity. Not the flat zero of complete dissociation.The productive middle: enough emotional engagement to generate motivation and meaning, calibrated enough that it does not flood the system.

That calibration is a physical skill. It lives in the body. And it is learnable.

The Body Keeps the Financial Record

Bessel van der Kolk, whose research on trauma and the nervous system produced the landmark book The Body Keeps the Score, documented something that applies well beyond the clinical context he was working in. The nervous system does not distinguish between emotional and physical experience at the level of storage. Early experiences of fear, threat, loss, and shame are encoded not only as narrative memories that can be consciously recalled, but as physical patterns: automatic responses in the nervous system that fire when similar stimuli appear, regardless of whether the narrative memory is consciously active.

For financial behaviour, this means something specific and practically important. The anxiety you experience when you open your bank account on a tense morning is not generated fresh from scratch each time you look. It is drawn from a bodylevel record of every previous time that financial engagement produced discomfort. The record was built from experiences you may or may not consciously remember: the household atmosphere when money was tight, the argument overheard, the purchase refused with a tension that a child registers even without understanding it, the adult memory of a debt or a shortfall or a financial decision that went badly. All of it is encoded physically, and all of it fires automatically when the relevant stimuli appear.

This is why purely cognitive approaches to financial anxiety are insufficient. You cannot think your way past a body-level response using the same cognitive system that the response has already partially compromised. The intervention must be physical: changing the state of the nervous system directly, through the body, before the cognitive consequences of the threat response have fully established themselves.

This is also why financial behaviour change often requires time and repetition rather than insight and resolution. The body-level record was built through accumulated experience. It is updated through accumulated experience. There is no shortcut to that accumulation, but there are practices that accelerate it, and they are the subject of this chapter.

Reading the Body's Financial Signals

The most useful financial skill this chapter teaches is not a technique. It is an awareness: the capacity to notice, with honest curiosity, what is happening in your body when financial material appears, before you have decided what to do about it and before the avoidance pattern has fully engaged.

Most people, when they pay attention, find that their body has been communicating clearly about financial stimuli for years. They simply have not been listening with sufficient attention to the signal. The chest tightening when a bank notification arrives. The slight shallowing of breath before opening an account balance. The jaw tension that appears at the thought of a salary conversation. The particular quality of heaviness in the stomach that accompanies the awareness that the quarterly investment review has been sitting undone for six weeks. These are not random sensations. They are the body's encoded record expressing itself in the present moment.

Developing the capacity to notice these signals changes their function. A physical sensation that is not noticed operates as a driver: it produces the avoidance response automatically, below the level of conscious choice. A physical sensation that is noticed and named operates as information: it tells you something about the state of your nervous system, which you can then choose to regulate before proceeding. The sensation is the same. Its relationship to your behaviour is completely different.

The practice of noticing is called a body scan, and it takes less than a minute. Before any financial task, pause. Take one breath. Direct your attention inward. Where in your body are you holding something? What is the quality of it, tight or loose, heavy or light, moving or still? Name it, one word is sufficient. You are not trying to resolve it or make it go away. You are simply acknowledging that it is there.

Research in somatic psychology and mindfulness consistently shows that the act of naming a physical sensation creates a small but real neurological shift: the activation of the prefrontal cortex's labelling function partially counteracts the amygdala's threat response. It does not eliminate the sensation. It changes the relationship between the sensation and the subsequent behaviour, creating the brief window of choice that was previously unavailable.

The Three-Breath Reset: The Most Useful Tool in This Book

Of all the practical tools in this book, the one that produces the most consistent and most immediate benefit is the simplest. Before you engage with anything financial, take three breaths with a deliberate extended exhale: four counts in through the nose, six counts out through the mouth. Three full cycles. Fortyfive seconds in total.

The mechanism is anatomical. The extended exhale activates the vagus nerve, which is the primary pathway of the parasympathetic nervous system, the branch responsible for rest, recovery, and what physiologists call the relaxation response. An exhale that is longer than the inhale signals to the nervous system, through the vagus nerve's mechanoreceptors in the diaphragm and lungs, that the acute threat phase has passed and the emergency response can begin to de-escalate. Cortisol levels begin to drop. Heart rate decreases slightly. Prefrontal cortex activity begins to recover.

This is not speculation or metaphor. It is the measurable physiology of a well-documented nervous system response. The technique is used, in various forms, by surgeons preparing for high-stakes procedures, by military operators before highpressure decisions in the field, and by competitive athletes before critical performances. The mechanism that makes it useful in those contexts is identical to the mechanism that makes it useful before you look at your investment account on a difficult morning.

Forty-five seconds of deliberate breathing does something specific and does not do. It does not produce calm in any complete sense. It does not eliminate the financial anxiety. It changes the neurochemical environment enough that the prefrontal cortex has meaningful participation in what follows, rather than operating in the compromised state that a full amygdala threat response produces. That partial recovery of analytical capacity is the difference between the automatic avoidance and the conscious choice to engage.

Use this technique before every financial engagement, without exception, for the first three months of building your practice. Not as an optional preliminary to the real work. As the first step of the real work, the step that makes every subsequent step more effective.

What Happens in the Body During the Spending Impulse

There is a specific application of somatic awareness that is particularly valuable for the Emotional Spender profile, though it is relevant to every profile at moments of financial stress. Understanding what is happening in the body during a spending impulse changes the relationship to that impulse in ways that cognitive understanding alone cannot produce.

Cortisol, elevated during the stress response, increases the brain's sensitivity to dopamine, the neurotransmitter most associated with reward, motivation, and the anticipation of pleasure. Under stress, the pull toward immediately available sources of dopamine becomes biochemically stronger.

In a consumer economy where almost anything can be purchased within seconds and delivered within hours, the spending impulse is one of the most accessible dopamine pathways available.

This means that when you are stressed and feel a strong impulse to purchase something, the impulse is not primarily about desire for the thing. It is about cortisol having sensitised your dopamine system and the dopamine system reaching for the most immediately available relief. The purchase provides a genuine, if brief, dopamine hit. The relief is real. The mechanism is neurochemical. The pattern is entirely learned and entirely changeable.

The intervention point is upstream of the purchase decision. By the time you are actively considering a specific purchase, the cortisol and dopamine dynamics are already well-established, and overriding them requires exactly the willpower that cortisol has compromised. The productive moment is earlier: the moment when you first notice the stress state in your body, before the spending impulse has formed.

Learning to ask, at that earlier moment, what do I actually need right now, changes the channel. The answer is almost never a purchase. It is usually something that addresses the actual stress: a few minutes of physical movement, a brief conversation with someone you trust, ten minutes of sitting outside, the acknowledgement that something is genuinely difficult right now. These alternatives are less immediately available than purchasing and produce a slower dopamine response. They also address the actual source of the discomfort rather than temporarily suppressing the signal while leaving the source intact.

The practice of pausing, noticing the physical quality of a purchase impulse, and asking what is actually happening in the body before acting on it is not a dietary restriction on spending. It is the development of a more accurate instrument for understanding your own states. Spending from genuine desire, with full awareness, is not the problem this chapter is trying to address. Spending as an automatic cortisol-management strategy is.

Building Your Financial Body Practice

The somatic financial practice I recommend is a three-step sequence that takes approximately two minutes and is applied before every financial engagement. Every account check. Every payment. Every investment review. Every money conversation. No exceptions, at least in the first three months.

Step one is a physical pause. Before opening any financial account or beginning any financial task, stop for thirty seconds. Do nothing. This pause is not wasted time. It is the transition between the cognitive state you were in a moment ago and the deliberately regulated state you are building. In the early weeks of this practice, this thirty-second stop will feel unnecessarily slow. That feeling is accurate information about how rarely you have been pausing before financial engagement. The pause is the point.

Step two is the three-breath reset: four counts in, six counts out, three full cycles. Forty-five seconds. Cortisol begins to drop. Prefrontal cortex function begins to recover. You are changing the biochemical conditions of the subsequent engagement.

Step three is the body scan: sixty seconds of directed attention to whatever is present in your body. Where is the tension? What is its quality? Name it. One word. You are not resolving it. You are mapping the territory so that it functions as information rather than as an automatic driver. Then engage with the financial task. From whatever state you are in after those two minutes, you engage. The goal is not the perfect calm of complete regulation, which is neither achievable nor necessary. The goal is the partial recovery of prefrontal cortex function that makes the difference between an automatic avoidance response and a conscious choice. That difference, accumulated across hundreds of financial engagements over months and years, is what changes the body's financial record.

Consistency matters more than perfection here. Two minutes of preparation before every financial engagement, even if some of those engagements still feel uncomfortable, builds the new neural pathways more effectively than intermittent deep practice when conditions are ideal. The nervous system learns from repetition, not from occasional intensity. Show up every time, even imperfectly. That is what changes the record.

Two minutes. Every time. That is the practice. The rest follows.

None of this is dramatic. That is precisely the point. Wealth building that is sustainable does not look dramatic from the inside. It looks like a two-minute practice before checking your accounts on a Sunday morning, sustained across six months of ordinary life. The drama, if there is any, shows up in the numbers over years, compounding quietly in the background of a life that has not been restructured around financial obsession but has simply incorporated a small, consistent, physiologically sound practice that keeps the financial engagement happening rather than being perpetually deferred.

At six months, the compounding effect of consistent regulated engagement begins to show up not just in the changed quality of the practice itself but in the financial decisions it has been quietly enabling. The automated contributions that were set up in month two have run undisturbed through whatever the markets have done. The salary conversation that happened in month three went better than feared and the annual increase reflected that. The debt clearance that started in month one has moved the balance measurably. The net worth, tracked weekly in the Evidence Journal, is pointing in the direction it should be pointing.

Around the two-month mark, something shifts that is hard to describe without sounding more dramatic than it is. The financial engagement begins to feel like something you do rather than something you brace yourself to do.

The accounts are opened and the numbers are noted with something closer to the curiosity of a scientist reading a gauge than the bracing of a person approaching something threatening. The anxiety has not disappeared. Its quality has changed: from threat to effort, and effort is something humans manage every day without the nervous system treating it as an emergency.

In weeks three through six, the practice begins to feel less effortful and more habitual. The two minutes of preparation before financial engagement start to feel normal rather than artificially imposed.

Some of the financial tasks that were previously accompanied by significant physical anxiety begin to feel merely routine. Others are still difficult. The Evidence Journal is accumulating entries, and there is something quietly significant about reading back through a record of your own engaged competence.

In the first two weeks, the main experience is noticing. You notice how much tension you were carrying before financial tasks that you had previously not been aware of. You notice how automatic the avoidance impulse is.

You notice that the three-breath reset actually does something measurable to the physical sensation, even if the overall anxiety is still present. The noticing itself feels like progress because it is progress: you have moved from automatic response to observed response, and that shift, however small it feels, is the foundation of everything that follows.

Most people who begin the somatic financial practice described in this chapter report a similar progression, and knowing it in advance makes it easier to persist through the early weeks when the practice feels effortful and the benefit is not yet felt.

What Changes, and When

The Evidence Journal: Writing the New Record

There is one more tool in this chapter that I want to describe before we move to Part Three's practical frameworks, because it operates at the same body-level where the financial record was built and where it needs to be updated.

The Evidence Journal is a written record of financial engagements completed and what actually happened when they were completed. Its format is simple: the date, the action taken, what you expected or feared before taking it, and what actually happened afterward.

Most of the time, what actually happens when you engage with financial material is not catastrophic. The account balance is what it is. The number, even if uncomfortable, is manageable. The investment account continued to exist. The salary conversation happened and the relationship survived. The debt payment went through and the balance decreased. These outcomes sound trivial in description and are not trivial in their neurological effect: each one is a piece of evidence that contradicts the threat prediction the amygdala has been operating from.

Written evidence persists where felt experience fades. The threat prediction your nervous system runs is maintained by accumulated historical evidence. The counter-evidence that updates it needs to be accumulated with similar persistence, and the Evidence Journal is the mechanism that makes that accumulation durable. When the Wealth Lock Loop reactivates, as it periodically will throughout any genuine engagement with financial change, reading back through your own record of competence is more convincing than any external reassurance could be. You were there. You know it is true. Start the journal this week. The first entry does not need to describe a dramatic financial action. It can describe looking at one account balance and noting that nothing terrible followed. That is sufficient. That is, in fact, the perfect beginning.

The body that holds your financial history can learn a new one. It learns through experience. The practices in this chapter are how you begin giving it different experiences to record.

Two minutes. Every time. That is the practice. The Evidence Journal makes it durable. Chapter Seven explains where the physical record of financial anxiety originally came from.

2.3 The Money Story You Were Given

The inherited beliefs running your financial life, and how to write a new chapter

"The greatest revolution of our generation is the discovery that human beings, by changing the inner attitudes of their minds, can change the outer aspects of their lives"

- *William James*

Over the years, a certain conversation keeps happening, in various forms, with more people than I can count over the years, and it almost always begins the same way.

Not with a question about investment strategy or debt management or salary negotiation. It begins with a pause, usually after we have been talking about financial patterns for a while, and then with a sentence that starts with the words: 'In my family, money was...'

What follows that sentence is different every time. In my family, money was never talked about. In my family, money was always a source of tension. In my family, we never had enough, and the adults around me carried that as a kind of permanent weather. In my family, money was something that other kinds of people had, not people like us. In my family, wanting more than you needed was considered a form of moral failure. In my family, the person who handled the money handled everything, and the rest of us were not supposed to need to know.

Every one of these sentences describes a financial education. Not the formal kind, not anything anyone sat down to teach deliberately. The kind that happens through absorption: through the atmosphere of a household, through what is said and what is pointedly not said, through what you watched the adults around you do and avoid and fear and pursue. Long before you earned your first salary, you had a fully formed relationship with money. You just did not choose it.

This chapter is about bringing that relationship into conscious view, because you cannot evaluate something you cannot see. And you cannot change something you have not evaluated.

The Research Behind the Scripts

The financial psychologists Brad Klontz and Ted Klontz spent years building what they called the money script framework: a taxonomy of the core beliefs about money that most people carry below the level of conscious thought and that exert consistent influence over financial behaviour regardless of income, education, or professional sophistication.

Their starting point was a clinical observation. In their work with individuals and families struggling with financial difficulties, the same patterns kept appearing across very different demographic groups. People who earned well were sometimes financially chaotic. People who earned modestly were sometimes quietly building genuine security. The financial outcomes did not correlate as strongly with income or knowledge as conventional wisdom suggested. They correlated more strongly with a set of underlying beliefs that operated automatically, before reasoning had a chance to engage.

Klontz and Klontz identified four primary categories of money script. The first they called money avoidance: the deep belief that money is inherently corrupting, that wealth is obtained at the expense of others, or that wanting financial success is a form of moral failing. The person running this script will often unconsciously limit their earning or wealth-building, because financial success does not feel safe at the identity level. They may be working very hard professionally while simultaneously ensuring that the outcomes of that work do not exceed a certain threshold of financial comfort, because exceeding it would mean becoming someone they have been taught to distrust.

The second category is money worship: the belief that more money will resolve most problems, that happiness and security are primarily functions of financial accumulation, and that the right level of wealth, once achieved, will produce a felt experience of arrival. The person running this script is often highly motivated financially but finds that reaching financial targets does not produce the satisfaction the script promised. The target recedes. The achievement feels hollow. The accumulation continues because stopping feels more dangerous than the emptiness of the constant pursuit.

The third is money status: the equation of net worth with personal worth, of financial position with social standing, of what you have with who you are. This script produces a particular relationship with money in which financial decisions are organised partly around display rather than utility, in which keeping up with the financial appearance of peers becomes a significant driver of spending, and in which genuine financial security is repeatedly sacrificed for the performance of financial security.

The fourth, and for our purposes the most common and consequential, is money vigilance: the belief that money is perpetually precarious, that financial security is always potentially temporary, that relaxing the vigilance around money is a form of dangerous naivety. The person running this script may have excellent financial habits in some respects, the careful attention to detail that vigilance produces, but they carry a chronic background anxiety about money that does not respond to the actual state of their finances. They can be objectively secure and still feel perpetually on the edge of not having enough. The nervous system learned 'not enough' in a context where that was true, and it has not updated the prediction for the context where it is no longer true.

A Story About Inheritance

During my time at ITC, in the early years of my career when I was still learning more about the sales business than I was contributing to it, I worked alongside a colleague I will call Prashant. He was a few years older than me, had been at the company longer, and was by any measure a strong performer. His territory numbers were good. His distributor relationships were well-maintained. His manager respected him.

We talked a lot in those years, the way you do when you are both young professionals finding your feet in a demanding first real job, and money came up often, usually in the oblique way it does when nobody has quite named it as the subject yet. Over time I understood something about Prashant that explained a pattern I had noticed in him professionally.

He was reluctant, in a way that seemed disproportionate to the evidence, to take any action that might result in visible failure. He would hold back from proposing a new distribution strategy even when his analysis was clearly sound, because if the strategy failed, the failure would be attributed to him. He would understate his achievements in reviews because overstating them and then not delivering felt catastrophically risky. He operated with a kind of pre-emptive self-limitation that had nothing to do with his actual capabilities.

One afternoon, in a tea stall between market visits, he mentioned something about his father. His father had run a small business for twenty years, worked hard, done well enough, and then lost most of what he had built in a single bad year when a major client defaulted. The family had gone from relative comfort to genuine strain almost overnight. Prashant had been twelve.

He did not connect the story to his current behaviour. It was just something that had happened in his family. But from that afternoon, I understood what was running underneath his professional hesitation. His nervous system had learned, at twelve, that what you build can disappear with unexpected speed. The script it had encoded was: do not build too visibly, because visible things can be taken. It had made perfect sense in the context of a twelve-year-old watching his father's world contract. It was costing him now, not in any dramatic way, but in the steady accumulation of opportunities not quite taken, risks not quite accepted, salary conversations not quite had.

I am not certain Prashant ever connected those dots. I did not say anything at the time, partly because I was twenty-three and had no framework for the connection, and partly because these things are difficult to say to anyone without it sounding like amateur psychology.

What I carry from that afternoon, though, is a clear understanding of something I have since seen confirmed many times in many contexts: the money story from childhood does not stay in childhood. It comes to work. It sits in the salary conversation. It shapes the investment behaviour. It runs quietly in the background of every financial decision, influencing outcomes in ways that look from the outside like choices but from the inside feel like simple reality.

Universal Patterns in the Money Story

Every family has a money story, and while the specific content varies enormously across different cultures, class, backgrounds, and generational experiences, certain patterns recur with enough consistency to be worth naming.

The first is the money-and-virtue tension. In many cultural and religious traditions, there is a deep and rarely examined equation between financial restraint and moral character. The person who does not pursue wealth visibly is understood to have their priorities straight. The person who pursues it openly is suspected of misaligned values.

This equation, absorbed early and held at the level of identity, creates a genuinely difficult internal conflict for the ambitious professional: the desire for financial success exists alongside the sense that genuinely wanting financial success is itself a character flaw. The conflict rarely resolves through conscious argument. It expresses itself in the pattern of building and then pulling back, of earning and not keeping, of knowing what to do and finding reasons not to do it.

The second pattern is the money-and-safety equation. For anyone who grew up in conditions of genuine financial precarity, or who witnessed a significant financial loss in the household during childhood, the nervous system has encoded a very specific prediction: financial security is unstable, what you have can be lost, comfort is the setup for a fall. This prediction can persist unchanged for decades after the circumstances that produced it have passed. The professional earning a solid salary and carrying this script may live, financially and emotionally, as though the salary could disappear at any moment, because that is what the body-level record says is true about money.

The third pattern involves money and identity within a community. For many professionals from working-class or immigrant backgrounds, or from any community defined in part by shared economic circumstances, financial success above the community norm carries a specific emotional weight. It can feel, at the level of identity, like separation.

Like becoming someone different from the people you love. Like acquiring a set of concerns and experiences that create distance rather than connection. This feeling is not paranoia. It sometimes reflects genuine social dynamics. But it can also produce a form of unconscious self-limitation: the pattern of not quite building past a certain level, because the body is managing the anticipated cost of going further.

None of these patterns were chosen. They were absorbed before there was enough life experience to evaluate them critically. The work of this chapter is not to condemn them or the people and circumstances that transmitted them. It is to surface them, because what can be seen can be examined, and what can be examined can, where it is not serving you, be changed.

Three Questions That Surface the Script

The most reliable method of identifying your operative money scripts is not analysis but honest self-inquiry. These three questions are designed to bypass the rational explanations that avoidance provides and reach the felt level where the scripts actually live.

The first: when you imagine achieving genuine financial security, not spectacular wealth but the specific condition in which your essential needs are reliably met, your future is adequately provided for, and an unexpected difficulty would not produce a crisis, what is the emotional quality of that imagination? Is it uncomplicated relief and satisfaction? Or is there something else alongside it? A slight sense of unreality, as though the imagined security belongs to a different category of person than yourself?

A vague anticipation of the thing that would go wrong? A foreboding about what security might cost? The emotional texture of your response to imagining security tells you what your nervous system predicts about it.

The second: when you think about the people who raised you, what would they feel, genuinely feel rather than what they would say, if they knew your exact financial position right now? Pride, relief, concern, quiet envy, validation of sacrifices they made, or perhaps a worry that you have moved too far from something they value? Anticipating those feelings does not mean they are determining your choices. But they may be influencing them in ways that have not been explicitly examined.

The third: is there any configuration of financial success that you find, in yourself or in others, morally uncomfortable? Not the dramatic versions, not the exploitative or dishonest paths to wealth. The ordinary ones.

Earning significantly more than your parents earned at your age. Accumulating savings that exceed what most people in your community have. Making financial decisions that prioritise your own household's security over family obligations that you have absorbed as your responsibility. Noticing that something in these scenarios produces resistance is important information about where a script is active.

The answers to these three questions are your money scripts. Not your financial opinions, which can be changed by argument. Your financial convictions, which can only be changed by experience. The difference matters because it points toward the correct intervention.

How Scripts Change: The Experience-Based Update

Here is the piece of this that most people most want to skip, because it is not the answer they are hoping for: money scripts do not change through insight.

Understanding your script clearly, tracing it to its origins, recognising exactly how and where it was formed, is genuinely valuable. It is not sufficient. You can have complete intellectual clarity about a money script and still run it automatically in every financial decision, because the script is not stored in the intellectual system. It is stored in the body-level implicit memory that Chapter Six described: the pattern that fires automatically when familiar stimuli appear, regardless of what the conscious mind knows about it.

Scripts change through accumulated contradicting experience. Specifically, through the repeated experience of actions that contradict the script's prediction without the predicted consequence following.

The script that says financial success leads to loss begins to update when financial success accumulates and loss does not follow, repeatedly, over time. The script that says people like us do not have wealth begins to update when the investment account grows, slowly and consistently, into something that demonstrably belongs to someone like you. The script that says wanting more is morally suspect begins to update when wanting more and acting on it does not produce the moral degradation the script predicted.

This is slow. It is not linear. There are periods when old scripts reassert themselves with full force despite months of contradicting experience, particularly under stress, when the nervous system returns to the most deeply encoded patterns as a form of homeostasis. This is normal and expected and does not mean the update has failed. It means the update is not yet complete.

The practices in Part Three of this book are designed, among other things, to generate the specific kinds of experience that update the most common wealth-limiting scripts. The automated investment that runs for six months without catastrophe following updates the safety script. The salary conversation that happens and produces a result updates the worth script. The net worth calculation that shows a positive trajectory updates the identity script. Each update is small.Together, over months and years, they shift the body-level record from which the scripts draw their power.

The money story you were given was someone else's, formed in circumstances that were not yours to choose. The story you are living now is the one being written by your current choices. This chapter is about understanding the first clearly enough to write the second deliberately.

A Practical Starting Point

Here is the Before moving to the next chapter, I want to offer one concrete action that takes less than twenty minutes and produces more useful self-knowledge than most financial planning exercises.

Write your family money story. Two pages, no editing, starting with the sentence: in my family, money was...

Write about the emotional atmosphere of your household around money. What was said, and what was conspicuously not said. Who handled the money, and what that meant for everyone else. What you absorbed about who deserves wealth and who does not. What you understood, without anyone telling you directly, about what financial success would mean for someone from your family.

Then read back what you have written and identify two or three sentences that feel like beliefs you are still carrying. Not historical observations. Active convictions. Write those sentences on a separate page and next to each one write: is this still true in my current reality? What evidence do I have that it is, or is not? What experience would update it?

That exercise does not change anything by itself. But it makes the invisible visible. And visible patterns, held with honesty rather than shame, are the ones that can be worked with.

The money story you were given was not chosen. The one being written now is. Chapter Eight examines the subtler, more recently formed patterns that have been building on that inherited foundation.

2.4 The Growth Blockers

he hidden patterns that limit financial progress without looking like problems

"The chains of habit are too light to be felt until they are too heavy to be broken"

- *Warren Buffett*

The most expensive financial patterns rarely look expensive from the inside.

They look like caution. They look like prudence. They look like knowing your limitations and not getting ahead of yourself. They carry the surface appearance of responsible adult financial behaviour, which is part of what makes them so effective at limiting financial progress over time. You cannot address what you cannot see, and growth blockers are masters of camouflage.

This chapter names four of them with enough precision that you can recognise them in your own financial life. Not as abstract tendencies to guard against, but as specific, observable patterns with specific, calculable costs and specific, practical interventions.

Growth Blocker One: The Wealth Ceiling

In 1986, a thirty-one-year-old woman I will call Elena started her first management role after several years in operational positions. Her salary increased meaningfully. For the first time in her working life, she had genuine surplus at the end of the month rather than the carefully managed shortfall she had been navigating since university.

She opened a savings account and started putting money into it with real intention. Within eight months, the account had grown to a figure that felt significant. She was proud of it. And then, over the next four months, a series of individually reasonable events reduced the balance almost entirely back to where it had started. A holiday that had been planned but whose cost expanded. A home improvement that was genuinely needed. A contribution to a family situation that felt obligatory. A car repair.

None of these expenses was extravagant. None was the result of poor planning. Viewed individually, each was defensible and many were unavoidable. What was striking was the pattern: each time the savings account approached a particular threshold, something happened to bring it back below that threshold. The same sequence repeated three times over four years, at approximately the same level each time.

Elena had a wealth ceiling. Not a conscious one, not a deliberate limitation she had imposed on herself. A nervous system-level ceiling: the level at which accumulated savings began to feel meaningfully different from the financial baseline her childhood had encoded as normal. When savings approached that level, her system generated an impulse to return to baseline. The rationalisations it found were always plausible, because they always were plausible. The pattern underneath them was always the same.

The wealth ceiling phenomenon was documented extensively by financial therapist Brad Klontz and has been replicated in subsequent research on self-sabotage in financial behaviour. Its mechanism is the one described in Chapter Two: the nervous system encoding a level of financial position as normal and generating discomfort, followed by corrective behaviour, when that level is significantly exceeded. The corrective behaviour looks like spending or generosity or practical necessity. It is, at the neurological level, homeostasis.

The ceiling is not the same for everyone. It tends to correspond to the financial level at which the person grew up, adjusted somewhat for the life they have since built. A professional whose family of origin was solidly middle-class may have a ceiling well above one whose family was working-class or poor, not because the professional is more financially capable but because the nervous system encoded a different baseline as normal.

Understanding the wealth ceiling as a pattern rather than a series of individual circumstances is the first step in addressing it. The second step is gradual extension: building savings to a level slightly above the ceiling, holding it there long enough for that level to encode as the new normal, then extending further. Not dramatically. Incrementally. The nervous system updates through repeated experience of a new level being safe, and that experience must be accumulated through time rather than asserted through will.

What This Looked Like in Practice

I recognised my own version of this pattern some years into my career. Not at the dramatic scale that Elena experienced, but in a subtler and, in retrospect, equally consistent form.

My ceiling was not a savings level. It was a decision level: a threshold of financial commitment above which I consistently found reasons for extended deliberation, additional research, one more thing I needed to understand before acting. Below that threshold, I was reasonably decisive. Above it, I would reliably spend weeks or months in the preparation loop that the next section describes. The threshold was real and specific, even though I had never consciously set it.

What I eventually understood was that the threshold corresponded, roughly, to the scale of financial decision that my parents had treated with visible anxiety when I was growing up. Decisions at that scale had carried emotional weight in my household. The nervous system had encoded that weight and was applying it automatically, regardless of whether my current financial position and capabilities made the same level of caution appropriate. It was not appropriate. But it felt, from inside the pattern, entirely reasonable.

This is the defining characteristic of the wealth ceiling: it feels like appropriate prudence from within it. The test is not whether the caution feels reasonable but whether it is consistent, whether it manifests at approximately the same level across different types of financial decision, and whether it has been maintained even when the objective financial circumstances that would warrant it have changed.

Growth Blocker Two: Preparation Infinity

There is a particular kind of financial non-doing that is exceptionally effective at disguising itself as doing. It involves research, it involves engagement with financial material, it produces a feeling of productive progress, and it generates, consistently, no actual financial action.

I call it Preparation Infinity. It is the research that has no natural endpoint because the requirement for more research is driven not by genuine knowledge gaps but by the anxiety of the action the research is supposedly preparing for. The research is not aimed at a decision. It is aimed at the perpetual deferral of the decision, in a form that provides psychological cover by appearing industrious.

The person in Preparation Infinity has spent six months reading about investment strategies without starting an investment. They have three notebook pages of notes on different index funds and have still not opened an account. They have researched salary negotiation tactics extensively and rehearsed the conversation multiple times in their head and have not yet scheduled the meeting with their manager. They know the theory completely. The theory is not the problem.

What distinguishes Preparation Infinity from genuine due diligence is the emotional quality of the preparation. Genuine due diligence is oriented toward a decision: it gathers specific information for a specific choice and stops when that information has been gathered.

Preparation Infinity is oriented away from the decision: it gathers information indefinitely, always finding one more thing that should be understood before the commitment can safely be made. The horizon of required preparation keeps receding as you approach it, because the preparation is not actually about being ready. It is about not yet having to be.

James Clear, in Atomic Habits, describes a similar pattern in the context of habit formation: the difference between motion and action. Motion is planning and researching and strategising. Action is the thing that actually produces an outcome. Motion feels like progress and is psychologically comfortable because it involves engagement without the vulnerability of commitment. Action is uncomfortable because it generates results that can be judged, and results that can be judged can be wrong.

The financial version of this distinction is stark. Motion is reading about investing. Action is investing. Motion is researching salary benchmarks. Action is having the salary conversation. Motion is understanding the tax code. Action is booking the appointment with the accountant and implementing the recommendations. Every month of motion rather than action has a specific, calculable cost. The Preparation Infinity pattern is, in aggregate, one of the most expensive financial behaviours available, precisely because it feels productive while producing nothing.

The unlock for Preparation Infinity is a decision rule, not a motivational intervention. Any financial action that has been in research phase for more than four weeks without a specific planned execution date is, by definition, in the loop.

The correct response is not more research. It is the smallest possible version of the action, taken this week. Not the perfectly designed investment portfolio. An account opened with any broadly appropriate fund, automated for any manageable amount, starting this month. Imperfect action taken now outperforms perfect action planned indefinitely, on the simple maths of compound growth.

The Nick Leeson Principle in Reverse

In 1995, a trader named Nick Leeson brought down Barings Bank, one of Britain's oldest financial institutions, through a series of unauthorised trades that accumulated losses of approximately 827 million pounds. The collapse became one of the most studied examples of financial disaster in modern banking history. What is less often discussed about the Leeson case is the institutional dynamic that enabled it: the extraordinary reluctance of Barings' management to look clearly at what was happening in the Singapore office, even when signals of serious problems were visible. The losses grew over eighteen months while senior management maintained a studied incuriosity about the detail. The discomfort of finding out was, apparently, managed by the comfort of not looking.

I raise this not to draw a direct comparison between Barings and an individual's financial avoidance, which would be disproportionate. I raise it because the dynamic is recognisable. The reluctance to look at something you suspect is going badly is not limited to failing financial institutions. It is a very common human response to the anticipation of uncomfortable information. And in personal finance, the cost of that reluctance, sustained over months and years, can be genuinely significant.

Preparation Infinity is, in a sense, the Nick Leeson principle in reverse: instead of hiding problems from oversight, it hides opportunity from action. The financial account that is never opened because the opening requires commitment. The salary that is never negotiated because the negotiation requires vulnerability. The debt that is never aggressively addressed because the full balance is never honestly calculated. The pattern of elaborate, energetic, purposeful not-looking.

The antidote, in both cases, is the same: looking. Directly, specifically, with the numbers in front of you rather than held vaguely in peripheral awareness. The discomfort of looking clearly is almost always less than the cost of the continued peripheral avoidance. And once you have looked, the specific action required is almost always more accessible than the vague dread of looking suggested it would be.

Growth Blocker Three: The Delegation Trap

The Delegation Trap is the pattern of handing off all financial engagement to someone else, a partner, a parent, a financial advisor, an accountant, and living, year after year, without independent understanding of your own financial position.

This arrangement feels efficient. One person is more comfortable with financial detail than the other, so the comfortable person handles it and the uncomfortable person is relieved of a source of anxiety. In practice, it works reasonably well until the conditions that made it work change: the relationship ends, the partner dies or becomes incapacitated, the advisor leaves, the accountant retires. At that point, the person who has been living in financial delegation discovers they have no map of their own financial life and no capacity to navigate it without the person who is no longer there.

I have had several conversations over the years with people, women more often than men though not exclusively, who found themselves in exactly this situation after a divorce or bereavement. The emotional difficulty of those events was already significant. The financial difficulty of discovering, in the middle of that emotional difficulty, that they had no idea what accounts existed, what the investment strategy was, or even where the insurance documents were kept, compounded it in ways that were entirely avoidable.

The distinction I want to draw is between delegation and abdication. Delegation says: you manage the operational detail, and I stay informed about the overall picture, understand the strategy, and participate in major decisions. That is a sensible division of labour. Abdication says: you handle all of it, and I prefer not to engage with any of the details. That is a vulnerability. The difference is not about who does the work. It is about whether both people maintain independent financial literacy.

The minimum standard of financial partnership, the level below which genuine financial vulnerability begins, is this: both people should be able to describe the complete household financial picture without referring to the other. Every account. Every debt. Every investment. Every insurance policy. The broad strategy and the approximate numbers. This is not a demand for equal operational involvement. It is the minimum condition for not being entirely dependent on another person's continued availability to navigate your own financial life.

The practical steps are straightforward, though they require the more financially engaged partner to be willing to share rather than to manage. A joint financial inventory review, once a year. Both names on accounts where possible. A shared document with account numbers, institution names, and the location of relevant documents. A single conversation every six months where both people describe the current financial position, in their own words, to each other. Small habits. Significant protection.

Growth Blocker Four: The Velocity Illusion

The human brain evolved for a world in which consequences followed causes within hours or days. Plant something, eat it. Hunt something, cook it. Build something, live in it. The feedback loop between action and outcome was tight enough to be directly perceived, and the ability to track cause and effect in that tight loop was a genuine survival advantage.

Compound growth operates on a completely different timescale. The most significant consequences of a financial decision made at thirty do not become visible until fifty or sixty. The monthly investment that makes a negligible visible difference to today's account balance is building, invisibly and with mathematical certainty, toward a figure that will matter enormously in three decades. The nervous system cannot feel this importance because the nervous system was built for the short loop, not the thirty-year loop.

The result is what I call the Velocity Illusion: the consistent, systematic undervaluing of financial actions whose most important consequences are temporally distant. The investment feels less urgent than it mathematically is because its payoff is invisible. The debt payment feels less important than it mathematically is because the interest it saves accrues silently rather than appearing as a felt benefit. The salary negotiation feels less worth the discomfort than it mathematically is because the compounding effect on lifetime earnings is an abstraction rather than a present experience.

Meanwhile, the financial actions with immediate consequences, the purchase that produces instant satisfaction, the avoidance that produces immediate relief, the debt minimum that resolves the month's cash flow, feel appropriately urgent because their consequences arrive in the feedback loop the nervous system is calibrated for.

This is not irrationality. It is the rational behaviour of a nervous system operating in an environment it was not designed for. The mismatch is architectural, and architectural problems require architectural solutions.

The primary architectural solution to the Velocity Illusion is the one this book returns to repeatedly: automation. When the monthly investment happens automatically, the nervous system does not need to feel its importance in order for it to occur.

The decision was made once, at a moment of clear longterm thinking, and the action happens regardless of how the nervous system is calibrated in any given month. The Velocity Illusion does not get to vote because the decision it would prevent has already been made and systemised.

The secondary solution is explicit calculation. The Opportunity Audit in Chapter Four is, in part, a tool for overcoming the Velocity Illusion: it converts the thirty-year consequence into a present number that the nervous system can actually perceive.

When you can see, as a specific figure, what this month's deferral costs in compounded future terms, the abstraction becomes concrete enough to act on. The calculation does not change the nervous system's architecture. It provides the information in a form the architecture can work with.

Recognising Your Primary Blocker

Most people, reading through these four patterns, will recognise one with greater clarity than the others. That primary blocker is worth naming specifically and sitting with honestly, because named patterns are addressable and unnamed patterns continue to operate freely.

The wealth ceiling manifests as a consistent inability to build savings or investments past a particular level, despite genuine intention and adequate income. The evidence is in the pattern over time: the same level approached, the same retreat, different reasons each time.

Preparation Infinity manifests as a specific financial action that has been in research or planning phase for more than four weeks with no scheduled execution date. The evidence is in the duration: how long has this been on the list, and what specifically is preventing the start?

The delegation trap manifests as an inability to describe your own complete financial picture independently. The evidence is immediate: try it now. Can you name every account, every debt, every investment, every insurance policy, and the approximate figures attached to each? If not, there is a delegation gap.

The velocity illusion manifests in the ratio of financial attention between the immediate and the long-term. If you can tell someone your monthly spend on discretionary categories but not the current balance of your retirement account, the velocity illusion is likely organising your financial attention.

Naming the primary blocker does not solve it. It makes the specific intervention visible. And specific interventions, applied consistently to specific patterns, change those patterns. That is what Part Three is designed to provide.

The growth blockers are patterns of mind. The patterns in the next chapter are patterns of relationship, and they are the ones most likely to be invisible precisely because they involve someone else.

2.5 The Wealth and the People You Love

Why money conversations are relationship conversations, and how to have the real ones

"Coming together is a beginning. Staying together is progress. Working together is success"

\- *Henry Ford*

The most revealing financial document in any household is not a bank statement or a tax return.

It is the silence around money. What is never discussed. What is known but not acknowledged. What both people feel and neither person names. In my experience of talking with people about their financial lives, the households with the most significant financial difficulties are almost never the ones with the worst incomes or the worst markets. They are the ones with the widest gap between what is happening financially and what is being talked about.

Money is not a neutral subject in any relationship where lives are genuinely shared. It touches too many of the things that matter most: safety and freedom, power and autonomy, what kind of future is being built and whose vision of that future is governing the decisions. When those underlying concerns are not addressed directly, they find their expression through the financial conversation, or more precisely through the absence of it, and the costs of that absence accumulate quietly over years.

This chapter is for anyone who shares their financial life with another person. Its central argument is simple: the financial partnership that works is not the one that avoids financial conflict. It is the one that has learned to have the real conversation underneath the financial one.

A Study Worth Understanding

In 2012, researchers at Kansas State University published findings from a study of more than four thousand couples, examining the predictors of relationship dissolution across a range of factors. Financial disagreements emerged as the single strongest predictor of divorce, stronger than arguments about children, stronger than conflict about sex, stronger than disagreements about in-laws or lifestyle or values.

What the researchers were careful to note is that this was not a finding about the financial situation itself. Couples with significant financial difficulties were not more likely to separate than couples with fewer difficulties, all else being equal. What predicted separation was the conflict around money, specifically the quality and recurrence of financial arguments, regardless of the underlying financial position.

The interpretation that makes most sense of this finding, and that aligns with what clinical work on money and relationships consistently shows, is that financial arguments are almost never really about money. They are about money as the medium through which the most fundamental relationship questions get expressed. Whose priorities govern shared decisions? Who has authority over the resources that both people depend on? What does the future look like, and whose version of that future is the one being built toward? These questions can be experienced directly and discussed explicitly, or they can be avoided and expressed sideways through arguments about specific financial decisions. The sideways version is more painful, less productive, and more likely to be repeated.

The Argument

That Is Never About the Number I want to describe a type of conversation that most couples who have been together for more than a few years will recognise, because naming it clearly is the first step to handling it differently. The conversation starts with a specific financial question. Whether to make a particular purchase. How much to spend on a holiday. Whether to increase the monthly investment or maintain it at the current level. Whether to help a family member financially. Both people have a position on the specific question. They make their cases. The cases are not unreasonable on either side. The conversation escalates anyway. Within a few minutes, the conversation is no longer about the specific question. One person is defending their fundamental right to make decisions about their own financial life. The other is arguing that the household cannot afford the kind of thinking that ignores consequences. One is saying that the other controls everything. The other is saying that the first one never takes responsibility for anything. The specific question is still technically on the table but neither person is actually arguing about it anymore.

What happened is that the financial question activated the underlying concerns that have never been directly addressed. The question of the holiday cost is actually the question of who has authority in this household. The question of the family contribution is actually the question of whose obligations take priority. The question of the investment level is actually the question of whose vision of the future is governing how shared resources are used. These questions are real and important and the relationship cannot fully function while they remain unexamined. But they are not being addressed. They are being fought about through proxy.

The proxy fight has a characteristic quality: both people feel misunderstood, both feel the other person is being unreasonable, and both are right. They are misunderstood, because the real subject is not what is being discussed. The solution is not to argue about the specific financial question more skillfully. It is to recognise the proxy fight for what it is and move the conversation to the level where the real question lives.

Three Misalignments That Drive Most Financial Conflict

In my observation of professional couples navigating financial decisions, almost all the recurring friction traces back to one of three underlying misalignments. These are not character incompatibilities and they do not predict relationship failure. They are differences in how each person's nervous system learned to relate to money, formed before the relationship began and brought into the shared life without examination.

The first is the safety-freedom split. One partner's primary financial orientation is toward security: building buffers, reducing risk, ensuring that a bad period would not produce catastrophe. The other's orientation is toward present-tense living: using money to fund experiences and quality of life now, rather than deferring all enjoyment for a future that is not guaranteed. Both orientations are rational responses to different histories and different value hierarchies. Both produce opposing financial instincts that surface in almost every significant financial decision.

The safety-oriented partner sees the holiday booking as a threat to financial resilience. The freedom-oriented partner sees the refusal to book it as a capitulation to anxiety at the expense of life. Both are describing the same situation from internally consistent positions. The conflict is not between a sensible person and an irresponsible one. It is between two people who have encoded different answers to the question: what is money for?

The second misalignment is the visibility gap. One partner wants full transparency about the household's financial position, regular updates, shared access to all accounts, joint involvement in all decisions. The other prefers to delegate financial management and not engage with the detail. This arrangement often develops naturally and unintentionally over the early years of a relationship, with neither person making a deliberate choice about it. One person is simply more comfortable with financial engagement and gradually takes on more of it, until the division of labour has become an information asymmetry: one person holds the complete picture, the other operates with partial knowledge of their own financial life.

The visibility gap produces a specific vulnerability. The uninformed partner has no independent basis for evaluating whether the decisions being made on their behalf are sound ones, no capacity to navigate without the informed partner if circumstances change, and no framework for contributing meaningfully to major financial decisions because they lack the information required to evaluate the options. The arrangement that felt like a sensible division of labour is functioning as a dependency.

The third misalignment is the present-future tension. One partner's financial decisions are consistently oriented toward current quality of life. The other's are consistently oriented toward future security. In the short term, this produces friction over specific decisions. Over a decade, it can produce a household that is neither fully enjoying the present nor adequately prepared for the future, because the two orientations are pulling resources in opposite directions without a shared framework for resolving the tension.

A Scene From the Field

During my time in a regional role at Marico, I worked closely with a sales manager and his wife who were both professionals with solid incomes and a genuinely difficult financial life that had nothing to do with either their earnings or their individual financial competence.

He was a natural saver, instinctively cautious, with a tendency to treat any discretionary spending as a potential threat to a security that had been hard-won. She was generous and present-tense in her financial orientation, more comfortable spending on experiences and family than on accounts she could not see growing. Both were sensible people. Their financial arguments were legendary in their social circle for their regularity and their intensity.

What I observed, in conversations with each of them separately over about eighteen months, was that neither of them understood what the other was actually managing. He did not understand that her spending was partly an expression of the fact that she did not feel heard in any conversation about money, so spending became the one financial domain where she felt she had agency. She did not understand that his vigilance was not about distrust of her but about a deep-seated fear, rooted in watching his father lose a business, that what you build can disappear, and that the only protection against that disappearance was constant watchfulness.

Neither of them had told the other these things, because they had not yet told themselves these things with enough clarity to put them into words. Their financial arguments were proxy fights for the conversations they had not yet learned to have.

They eventually had those conversations. Not in a single dramatic session but over a period of months, sometimes prompted by a specific argument, sometimes more deliberately. What changed was not their financial positions, which were already fine. What changed was the quality of the financial decision-making, which became something they did together rather than something each person did against the resistance of the other.

Four Conversations That Change the Financial Partnership

These four conversations are not a curriculum or a programme. They are a sequence that builds on itself: each one creates the conditions that make the next one possible. They should be held separately, with time between them, rather than compressed into a single session. The first conversation is about history. Each person shares their family money story, as described in Chapter Seven, not to justify current behaviour but to make it comprehensible. The goal of this conversation is a specific sentence: I now understand why you have the financial responses you do, even when they are different from mine. That sentence, meant and felt rather than just said, changes the emotional foundation of every subsequent financial discussion.

The second conversation is about current reality. Together, both people map the complete household financial picture. Every account. Every debt.

Every asset. Every income source. Every insurance policy. Both people should emerge from this conversation able to describe the complete picture independently, without reference to notes or to each other. If either person cannot, the conversation has not yet gone far enough. This is not a punitive standard. It is the minimum condition for genuine financial partnership.

The third conversation is about vision. Each person writes, separately before they compare, their answers to three questions: What does financial security feel like, as a lived experience rather than a number? What do you most want money to enable in the next ten years? What does enough look like for you, specifically? The comparison of the separatelywritten answers, held with genuine curiosity rather than the expectation of agreement, reveals the actual alignment and misalignment. From the overlap, a shared vision can be built. From the divergence, an explicit negotiation can begin, rather than the implicit one that has been happening through proxy fights.

The fourth conversation is about operating structure. Based on what the first three conversations have revealed, both people agree on how financial management will actually work: who manages which accounts operationally, what level of decision requires joint discussion, how each person maintains independent financial literacy, and when the household will review its financial position together. This is not a contract. It is an agreement that both people have authored rather than one person having imposed on the other, which means both people are more likely to honour it.

On Different Financial Profiles in a Shared Life

One of the most consistent patterns in couples who struggle financially is the pairing of complementary but conflicting wealth profiles. The Deferrer and the Control Architect. The Vigilance Trapper and the Emotional Spender. The pairings often have an unconscious logic, we are drawn to people whose orientation in the world balances or completes our own, but in the financial domain they create specific and predictable friction.

The Control Architect's operational rigidity activates the Deferrer's withdrawal. The Vigilance Trapper's monitoring amplifies the Emotional Spender's anxiety and therefore their spending response. Each person's pattern, in the presence of the other's, becomes slightly more entrenched than it would be alone.

The insight that changes this dynamic is the same one that appears throughout this book: your partner's financial behaviour is not a deliberate choice to undermine the household's financial goals. It is their nervous system's automatic response to its history, running the pattern it learned before you knew each other and applying it to a shared life you are now trying to build together. Understanding this, with genuine rather than performed empathy, shifts the relationship from opposition to collaboration. And collaboration, sustained over years, builds wealth that opposition cannot.

Part 3

ACTIVATE YOUR WEALTH

The specific practices that close the gap between knowing and doing

3.1 The Clarity Foundation

Building the baseline from which every financial improvement becomes possible

"For every minute spent organising, an hour is earned"

\- *Benjamin Franklin*

Most people approach financial behaviour change by beginning in the wrong place.

They begin with strategy. Which funds to invest in. How to structure the debt clearance. The most efficient tax approach. Whether to prioritise the emergency fund or the investment account. The strategy questions are real and the answers to them matter. But strategy applied in a dysregulated state, by a nervous system that has not yet built the physiological capacity to sustain financial engagement, produces at best inconsistent results and at worst the experience of having tried properly and still failed, which makes the next attempt harder.

The right starting point is not strategy. It is what I call the Clarity Foundation: a set of simple, repeatable practices that build the physiological and psychological baseline from which every other financial improvement in Part Three becomes possible. Not comfortable, necessarily. Possible: meaning the prefrontal cortex is sufficiently online, the threat response is sufficiently regulated, and honest engagement with the actual state of your financial life is sufficiently tolerable to be sustained week after week.

The Clarity Foundation has three elements. They are sequenced because that is how they build, each one making the next more accessible. But they are also mutually reinforcing: practising any one of them makes the others easier, and the combination is substantially more powerful than any element alone.

Why Sequence Matters

In 2010, a team of researchers at the University of Southern California published findings on what they called the willpower resource model: the observation that self-regulatory capacity, the ability to override impulses and maintain intended behaviour, is a finite resource that depletes through use and recovers through rest. Decision fatigue, as it came to be called in popular discussion, describes the real phenomenon of decision quality degrading as the cumulative cognitive load of decisions increases across a day or a week.

Applied to financial behaviour, the implication is important. The person who arrives at their financial practice after a long day of work and decision-making, opens their accounts in a state of cognitive depletion, and tries to make sound financial choices is asking their system to perform well under exactly the conditions that most reliably produce poor performance. They are not failing through lack of discipline. They are failing through a mismatch between the demands of the task and the state of the system attempting it.

The Clarity Foundation addresses this mismatch directly. Its first element, the physiological preparation, is not preliminary to the work. It is the first step of the work, the step that changes the conditions under which all subsequent steps occur. Done consistently, it builds a different baseline: a starting state from which financial engagement produces different results because the system doing the engaging is in a different condition.

Element One: The Weekly Financial Review

The single most important financial habit in this book is fifteen minutes, at the same time, on the same day, every week.

Not fifteen minutes of strategy. Not fifteen minutes of decision-making or planning or problem-solving. Fifteen minutes of pure, non-judgmental observation of where you currently are. Think of the way a ship's navigator takes a position fix: not to decide on a new course, not to adjust anything, simply to establish with precision where the ship is at this moment. The clarity of the fix makes every subsequent navigation decision more sound.

The structure of the fifteen minutes is deliberately specific, because structure removes the recurring decision about how to do it and that recurring decision is one of the places the Wealth Lock Loop finds its entry point.

The first three minutes are physiological preparation. Three-breath reset. Body scan. The preparation from Chapter Six, applied before opening any account. This is not optional. It is the condition that makes the remaining twelve minutes useful rather than anxiety-driven.

Minutes four through eleven are pure observation. Open every account: savings, checking, investment, retirement, credit. Note the balance of each. Calculate net worth: total assets minus total liabilities. Write the figure down with the date. Make no decisions. Apply no judgments. Note no should or should-nots. You are a scientist reading gauges, not a judge reviewing conduct.

Minutes twelve through thirteen are for one action. Not the most important action available. The most completable one: the financial task that has a clear beginning, a clear end, and can be finished within the week. Small enough to be done. Meaningful enough to matter.

Minutes fourteen and fifteen are for the Evidence Journal: one sentence recording what you observed, one word for how it felt, and what you committed to. The sentence is not a paragraph. The word is not a justification. The commitment is not a resolution. Just the date, the observation, the feeling, the action.

This practice sounds almost trivially simple. The reason I describe it in this level of detail is that simplicity is what makes it sustainable, and sustainability is what makes it effective. Financial practices that require complex setup or significant decision-making each time they are done get abandoned when life gets difficult. Financial practices that are simple enough to do in fifteen minutes, on the same day each week, regardless of how difficult life is, get maintained. And what gets maintained is what changes things.

The transformation this practice produces is not dramatic. After four weeks, the accounts feel slightly more familiar and slightly less threatening. After eight weeks, the weekly review feels routine rather than effortful. After twelve weeks, most people report something that surprises them: they look forward to it. Not with excitement. With the quiet satisfaction of a practice that has become comfortable enough to be genuinely informative rather than primarily anxiety-producing. The numbers are still the numbers. The relationship with the numbers has changed.

What Happened When I Started

I want to be honest about what my first few weeks of this practice looked like, because the polished description of the protocol as it is intended to work does not capture the actual experience of beginning it.

The first week, I did the three-breath reset and then sat for about forty seconds doing nothing while I tried to remember where I had all my accounts. I had more accounts than I had realised. Some of them I had not looked at in over a year. The net worth calculation produced a number that was not as bad as I had feared but was also not where I felt it should be, given how long I had been earning. I wrote one sentence in the Evidence Journal, felt moderately uncomfortable about the whole exercise, and was glad when it was over.

The second week was easier because the accounts were now known quantities. The discomfort was still present but had a different quality. Less like dread, more like effort. Effort is manageable.

By the sixth week, the fifteen minutes had become a genuine anchor in my week. Not because the practice had become emotionally neutral, the numbers still mattered and I still had preferences about their direction, but because the regularity of the observation had built something that was previously absent: a continuous relationship with my financial reality rather than the episodic, crisis-driven engagement that had characterised my previous financial life. I knew where I stood. Every week. That knowing changed how I made decisions throughout the week, not dramatically, but consistently.

The most significant change was the elimination of the background anxiety that comes from not knowing. The vague, persistent sense that the financial situation is probably worse than you are allowing yourself to look at is its own form of cognitive load. The weekly review replaced that vague anxiety with specific information. Specific information, even when the specific numbers are not what you would choose, is less cognitively exhausting than sustained vagueness.

Element Two: The Evidence Journal

The Evidence Journal is a written record of financial engagements completed and what actually happened when they were completed. Its format: the date, the action taken, what you expected or feared before taking it, and what actually happened.

Its purpose is to change what the amygdala predicts about financial engagement, by building a specific, personal, written record of the evidence that the prediction is wrong.

The amygdala's threat prediction about financial engagement was built through accumulated experience. It will be updated through accumulated experience. The Evidence Journal is the accumulation mechanism: it ensures that the counter-evidence generated by every completed financial action is recorded rather than fading, and available to be reviewed when the threat prediction reasserts itself, as it periodically will.

One practical point on the Evidence Journal that I have found makes a significant difference: the 'what actually happened' entry should be honest rather than positive. The goal is not to record that everything felt great. The goal is to record what actually occurred. Sometimes what actually occurs is that the account balance was lower than expected and that felt bad. Sometimes the investment review revealed an allocation that probably needs adjusting. Sometimes the salary conversation did not go as hoped. Recording these honestly, alongside the specific fact that you engaged with the material rather than avoiding it, is more useful than recording a sanitised version. The journal is evidence of engagement, not a highlights reel.

Over months, the Evidence Journal becomes something unusual in most people's experience: a written record of their own financial competence. Not dramatic competence. The competence of someone who looked at all their accounts every week and did not fall apart.

Who made one extra debt payment and saw the balance decrease. Who opened an investment account and left it alone through a period of market volatility. These feel small in the moment and are, in aggregate, the foundation of a different financial identity.

Element Three: The Financial Inventory

The Financial Inventory is a one-time comprehensive audit of your complete financial position. Every account with its balance. Every debt with its outstanding amount and interest rate. Every asset with its approximate current value. From these numbers, one figure: net worth.

Most people who have not done this exercise recently find either that the number is better than expected, because there were accounts and assets they had been mentally discounting, or that it is worse than expected, because there were debts and charges they had been avoiding seeing clearly. In either case, the value is identical: a clear, complete, honest picture of the starting line.

The Financial Inventory is not updated weekly. Net worth is updated weekly during the Financial Review, but the full inventory only needs to be redone annually, during the Annual Strategic Review described in Chapter Twelve. The weekly figure is sufficient for tracking trajectory. The full inventory is for establishing the baseline clearly and for the annual check of whether the complete picture has shifted in ways the weekly tracking does not capture.

Do the Financial Inventory with the physiological preparation from Chapter Six in place. The experience of encountering numbers you have been avoiding is genuinely activating, and the regulated state makes it possible to complete the exercise rather than close it halfway through when something uncomfortable appears. The three-breath reset before you open the first account is not optional preparation. It is the condition that makes honest completion possible.

The Practice in Real Life: What to Expect

Financial behaviour change does not progress smoothly. Expecting a linear improvement, week after week more comfortable and more effective, sets up a discouragement that is not warranted by how the actual process works.

The first two to four weeks of the Clarity Foundation practice are typically the most effortful. The accounts are newly engaged with, the discomfort is still near its peak, and the Evidence Journal does not yet have enough entries to provide meaningful counter-evidence to the threat prediction. This period requires the most discipline to sustain and produces the least felt reward. It is also the most important period, because continuing through it is the act that begins to change the neural prediction.

Weeks five through eight see a meaningful shift in the quality of the discomfort. It becomes less like threat and more like effort, and effort is something humans sustain routinely in domains they value. The accounts feel more familiar. The weekly review feels more like a habit and less like a confrontation. The Evidence Journal is accumulating entries that provide genuine counter-evidence when the old anxiety reasserts itself.

By month three, most people report that the weekly review has become the kind of comfortable routine that produces mild discomfort when it is missed rather than when it is done. The relationship with financial reality has changed at the level of habit rather than just intention. The foundation, built through thirteen weeks of consistent fifteen-minute practice, is solid enough to support the practical financial moves that Part Three's subsequent chapters describe.

Build the foundation first. Build it before the investment strategy and before the debt clearance plan and before the salary negotiation preparation. Everything in the chapters that follow will work better, persist longer, and survive disruption more reliably if it is built on this foundation rather than on the anxious, irregular, crisis-driven engagement that characterises most people's previous relationship with their financial lives.

3.2 The Compounding of Small Actions

Why the brain changes through small consistent steps, and how to use this

"A journey of a thousand miles begins with a single step"

- *Lao Tzu*

In 2003, the British national cycling team appointed Dave Brailsford as its performance director.

The team had not won an Olympic gold medal in seventy-six years. In professional road racing, British cyclists had never won the Tour de France. The results over the previous century were, by any reasonable assessment, unremarkable.

Brailsford introduced a philosophy he called the aggregation of marginal gains. The idea was straightforward: identify every element that contributes to cycling performance, improve each one by one percent, and let the aggregate of those small improvements compound into something significant. The team examined everything. The standard areas: training regimes, nutrition, aerodynamics. And the non-standard areas: the ergonomics of the bike seats, the type of massage gel that produced the fastest muscle recovery, which pillow design produced the best sleep quality in hotel rooms. They travelled with their own pillows.

Within five years, the team won sixty percent of the gold medals available at the 2008 Beijing Olympics. At the 2012 London Olympics, they dominated. And between 2012 and 2018, British cyclists won the Tour de France five times. Brailsford's principle has become one of the most cited ideas in performance psychology, and for good reason: it describes something true about how improvement actually works in systems that are both complex and human. Not through single dramatic interventions but through the accumulated compound of many small ones.

Financial behaviour change works the same way. Not because the metaphor is apt but because the underlying mechanism is the same: each small improvement changes the conditions for the next, and the compound of many small changes produces outcomes that no single dramatic intervention could have delivered.

Why Small Works Better Than Large

There is a neurological reason why starting small is not just psychologically easier but actually more effective than beginning with ambitious commitments, and it is worth understanding clearly because it runs counter to the intuition that significant goals require significant initial actions.

The threat response, described in Chapter Two, activates when an action feels overwhelming relative to current capacity. 'Start investing seriously' is a statement that feels overwhelming to someone who has not yet opened an investment account.

'Open an account with whatever minimum is required' is not overwhelming. The difference between those two phrasings is not just psychological comfort. It is the difference between an instruction that triggers the threat response and closes down the prefrontal cortex, and an instruction that stays below that threshold and allows the prefrontal cortex to remain engaged throughout the action.

BJ Fogg, the behaviour scientist at Stanford whose work on tiny habits has influenced the field significantly, makes a related point through what he calls the motivation wave: moments of high motivation produce an impulse to make large commitments, but large commitments made in moments of high motivation are rarely maintained when motivation returns to its normal level, because behaviour maintenance depends not on motivation but on habit formation, and habit formation requires repetition that is consistent enough to persist through lowmotivation periods.

The small action that is maintained consistently across both high-motivation and low-motivation periods is worth more, financially and neurologically, than the large commitment that is sustained during the motivation wave and abandoned two weeks later. This is not a counsel of low ambition. It is an accurate description of how habits form and how the brain changes.

James Clear's central argument in Atomic Habits, supported by extensive research in the psychology of behaviour change, is that identity change drives behaviour change rather than the reverse: the person who believes they are the kind of person who invests regularly will find the specific investment decision much easier than the person who is trying to force themselves to invest through will alone. And identity changes through accumulated evidence.

Small actions, completed reliably, generate the evidence that builds the identity. Large actions, undertaken once and then abandoned, generate a different kind of evidence: that attempts to change do not last.

The Graduated Practice Sequence

The sequence in which financial practices are introduced matters. Introducing a complex practice before the nervous system has built the baseline capacity to sustain it produces the experience of failure, which makes subsequent attempts harder. The sequence below is designed to build each capacity before adding the next.

In the first two to four weeks, the only practice is the Clarity Foundation from Chapter Ten. Nothing else. The weekly review, the Evidence Journal entries, and the Financial Inventory. These alone. The purpose of this period is to build the physiological and psychological baseline: the experience of regular financial engagement without catastrophe, the accumulated counterevidence in the journal, the clarity of the complete picture. Building this baseline is not preliminary to the real work. It is the first layer of the real work, and every subsequent layer depends on it.

In weeks five through eight, one automation is added. Not several. One. Whatever is most accessible and most consequential from the Clarity Foundation's inventory: the bill that could be on autopay and is not, the savings transfer that could be scheduled and is not, the investment contribution that could be automated and is not.

One action, set up once, running automatically. The value of this is not only financial. It is the experience of a financial change that, once made, continues to operate without requiring repeated acts of will. That experience is genuinely different from anything that requires recurring decision-making, and the difference is felt.

In months two and three, the automation architecture is extended gradually: a second automated action, then a third, building the layered system described in Chapter Twelve. And the first non-automated financial conversations begin: the first direct engagement with the debt balance and interest rates, the first research into market compensation, the first conversation with the relevant professional about structural efficiency.

From month three onward, the sequence adapts to the individual: the specific actions most relevant to the specific opportunity audit, in the order that the person's particular profile and circumstances make most accessible. The framework is consistent. The specific content varies.

A Story About Incremental Progress

When I was managing a sales team at Perfetti Van Melle during a particularly challenging market period, one of the lessons I learned from watching the territory managers navigate their targets was about the relationship between visible progress and sustained effort.

We were in a market where the big structural wins, the new distribution agreements, the major account conversions, were genuinely difficult and often took months to materialise. Some of the team members handled this well and maintained their effort and their morale through the long periods between visible wins. Others found the absence of dramatic progress demoralising and became less effective the longer the visible wins were delayed.

The managers who maintained their effectiveness were, almost without exception, the ones who had built practices that generated visible, small evidence of progress on a daily or weekly basis, independent of whether the large wins were materialising. They tracked outlet-level engagement. They noted small relationship improvements with retailers. They tracked their own activity metrics rather than only the outcome metrics. They had built, essentially, an evidence journal for their professional work: a record of the small, consistent, directional actions that were building toward the large outcome even when the large outcome was not yet visible.

The managers who struggled were the ones who could only evaluate their progress through the large outcomes, and when the large outcomes were delayed, they had no intermediate evidence of forward movement. The absence of visible progress felt like the absence of progress, which felt like failure, which made sustained effort psychologically more difficult.

Financial behaviour change has the same structure. The large outcomes, the meaningful investment balance, the significantly improved net worth, the cleared debt load, are real and they will materialise with sustained practice. But they materialise slowly.

The small outcomes, the automated contribution that ran this month, the one extra payment that reduced the debt balance by a measurable amount, the weekly review completed and recorded, these are the intermediate evidence that makes sustained effort psychologically possible. Write them down. Note them. The Evidence Journal exists, among other reasons, to give you what those territory managers had: evidence of forward movement even when the large outcome is not yet visible.

The Automation Architecture in Full

Automation is not a technique in this book. It is a philosophy. The central financial insight of this chapter and the next is that the most durable financial behaviours are the ones that have been removed from the domain of recurring decisionmaking and placed in the domain of automatic execution.

Every recurring financial decision is a recurring opportunity for the Wealth Lock Loop to activate. Every month that the investment contribution requires an active decision is a month where the Deferrer's pattern, the Vigilance Trapper's anxiety, the Emotional Spender's current emotional state, or the Control Architect's budget constraints can prevent the contribution from happening.

Automation removes the decision. When the decision is absent, the blocker has nothing to work with. The automation architecture is built in layers. The first layer is payment automation: every regular bill, premium, subscription, and minimum payment set to automatic execution.

This layer eliminates late fees, late payment anxiety, and the cognitive load of tracking what is due when. It costs nothing to implement and produces immediate psychological benefit in the elimination of an entire category of avoidable financial stress.

The second layer is savings automation: a fixed amount, transferred to a separately labelled account on the day after salary credit. The amount should be the honest answer to: what could I move without genuine hardship? Not the aspirational answer. The honest one. Start lower and increase it than start high and reduce it. Reduction signals defeat to the nervous system. Increase signals progress.

The third layer is investment automation: a regular contribution to whatever long-term investment vehicle is most appropriate for your situation. The specific vehicle matters less than the automaticity.

An automated contribution to a broadly appropriate fund, maintained through market volatility because it requires no monthly decision to maintain, outperforms the carefully optimised portfolio that requires monthly decisions to fund and therefore gets interrupted by the first difficult month.

Build these layers one at a time, stabilising each before adding the next. The complete architecture, built over three to four months, represents the single largest structural improvement most people can make to their financial life.

On the Difficulty of Starting

I want to close this chapter with something that is rarely said in books about financial behaviour but is, in my experience, consistently true: beginning is the hardest part, and the difficulty of beginning does not mean you are doing it wrong.

Starting something you have been meaning to start for a long time has a particular quality of difficulty something you have been meaning to start for a long time. It is not just the difficulty of the action itself.

It is the weight of the interval: the awareness that you have been intending this for months or years and that beginning now means acknowledging that the beginning did not happen sooner. That awareness can make beginning feel like a judgement as well as an action. It is not. It is just a beginning.

The compound curve of financial growth is patient. Starting at thirty-five rather than thirty is not catastrophic. Starting at forty rather than thirty-five is not catastrophic. Every starting point has a remaining horizon, and every remaining horizon has compound growth available within it.

The best starting point was earlier. The second-best starting point is now. That has always been true and remains true regardless of how long the interval before this moment was.

One step. Any step. Today. That is sufficient to begin the compounding of small actions. The rest follows from the beginning.

3.3 Five Wealth Activation Moves

The practical financial actions that produce the largest returns for real people in real lives

"The best time to plant a tree was twenty years ago. The second best time is now"

- *Chinese proverb*

Every piece of financial advice in the world can be reduced to a relatively small number of core actions. The challenge is never really knowing what to do.

The challenge is doing it. Which means the most useful financial guidance is not the advice that is most technically optimal but the advice that is most likely to be implemented by a real person managing real complexity: a job, a family, competing obligations, varying energy and emotional states, and the psychological patterns this book has spent eleven chapters describing.

The five moves in this chapter are selected on exactly that basis. Not because they are the only financial actions worth taking or the most sophisticated ones available. Because they consistently appear at the intersection of financial significance and psychological accessibility: they produce large financial benefits, and they are the ones that real people, with the understanding from Parts One and Two, can actually do and actually sustain.

Each move is presented with its financial case and its behavioral case. The financial case is what makes it worth doing. The behavioral case is what makes it possible to do. Both matter.

Move One: The Complete Financial Picture

Once complete, the inventory is not revised weekly. The net worth figure is tracked weekly during the Clarity Foundation review. The full inventory is redone annually. Between annual reviews, the weekly net worth figure does the work of tracking trajectory.

Do the Complete Financial Picture with the physiological preparation from Chapter Six. Three-breath reset before you open the first account. Body scan before you begin the calculation.

These are the tools that keep the experience below the threat threshold long enough to complete it honestly. Without them, many people find themselves closing the spreadsheet halfway through when the numbers become uncomfortable. With them, completion becomes possible.

The resistance to this step is real and worth addressing directly. Most people who have been inconsistently engaged with their finances suspect, at some level, that the complete picture is worse than they have been allowing themselves to see. The resistance to doing the inventory is partly the resistance to having that suspicion confirmed. This resistance is worth naming and then doing the exercise anyway, because the suspicion is almost always either inaccurate or less damaging than the sustained avoidance of knowing. Whatever the number is, it is the number you are working with. Not knowing it does not make it different. It just makes it unaddressable.

The Complete Financial Picture is your history. Every account, every debt, every asset, every obligation, documented in one place on one page with the date. The figure at the bottom is your net worth: total assets minus total liabilities. This figure becomes the single most important number in your financial practice, because it captures the combined effect of every financial decision you make and allows you to track the direction of travel rather than the fluctuation of any individual component.

Every physician, before proposing treatment, establishes a complete picture of the patient of the patient's current state. Not because the history is the treatment, but because sound treatment is impossible without it. The same principle applies in personal finance, and is almost universally ignored in favour of jumping directly to the action.

Move Two: The Automation Foundation

The single most powerful structural change most people can make to their financial life is not a new investment or a debt clearance plan or a salary negotiation. It is automating as much of their financial activity as possible.

This sounds undramatic. That is because it is undramatic. The drama in financial advice is usually about the large, visible, emotionally salient actions: the dramatic investment, the bold salary ask, the transformative financial plan. The unsexy truth is that automation, implemented consistently and left to run, produces more financial improvement over a decade than any number of dramatic actions taken and then inconsistently maintained.

The automation foundation has three layers, built sequentially. Layer one: every regular bill and minimum payment on automatic execution. Every insurance premium, utility bill, loan minimum, and subscription that can be set to auto-pay is set to auto-pay. This takes one afternoon to set up and eliminates, permanently, an entire category of financial anxiety and financial error. Late fees, damaged credit scores, and the cognitive load of tracking due dates are all products of manual bill management. Automation eliminates them.

Layer two: a fixed savings transfer on the day after salary credit. The amount should be the honest answer to the question asked in Chapter Eleven: what could I move consistently, every month, without genuine hardship? The transfer goes to a separately named account, Emergency Reserve, or Savings, or whatever label increases the psychological barrier to raiding it for non-emergency purposes. The label matters. Generic savings accounts get raided. Named accounts with explicit purposes have a higher psychological threshold.

Layer three: the investment contribution. This is the automation that produces the most significant long-term financial outcome. A fixed amount, invested in a broadly appropriate index fund or retirement vehicle, on an automated schedule that requires no monthly decision to execute. The specific fund is less important than the automaticity. An automated contribution to a reasonable fund, maintained through market volatility, will outperform the perfectly optimised portfolio that requires monthly decisions to fund, because monthly decisions are where the Wealth Lock Loop activates.

Build these layers in order, stabilising each before adding the next. The complete architecture takes three to four months to establish. Once established, it runs. And what it runs toward, every month, without requiring heroism or high motivation, is the compound curve of long-term financial growth.

Move Three: The Debt Sequence

For anyone carrying high-interest consumer debt, the most straightforward financial priority in their life is one that requires no market knowledge, no investment expertise, and no professional credentials to implement: eliminate that debt as aggressively as the budget allows.

The logic is simple and the numbers are unambiguous. Debt at twenty-two percent interest costs twenty-two percent per year. There is no widely available investment that offers a guaranteed twenty-two percent annual return. Eliminating the debt produces a guaranteed return equivalent to the interest rate. No stock market required. No market timing required. No risk of loss.

The method most supported by both financial mathematics and behavioural evidence is the avalanche approach: list all debts by interest rate, highest to lowest. Pay the minimum on every debt. Direct every available additional dollar to the highest-interest debt first. When it is cleared, redirect the full amount that had been going to it, minimums plus extra payments, to the next highest-interest debt. The cascade accelerates as each debt is eliminated because the available payment amount grows.

The alternative, the snowball approach of clearing the smallest balance first regardless of interest rate, costs more in total interest but produces the behavioural reinforcement of seeing a debt eliminated completely, which some people find sufficiently motivating to sustain the practice better than the mathematically superior avalanche. The best debt clearance strategy is the one that is actually followed for the months or years required to complete it. Mathematical optimality is only relevant if the strategy is maintained.

One practical note on the relationship between debt clearance and investment. The common question is whether to prioritise debt clearance or investment. The answer depends on the interest rate of the debt and the expected return of the investment. As a working principle: debt above ten percent interest should be prioritised over investment in most circumstances, because the guaranteed return of eliminating that debt exceeds the expected return of most diversified investment strategies over relevant time horizons. Debt below ten percent, particularly low-rate mortgages, need not necessarily be aggressively cleared in preference to investment. The specific calculation for specific situations is worth a conversation with a qualified financial professional.

Move Four: The Emergency Reserve

The emergency reserve is the financial practice that produces the largest behavioural return per dollar invested. Not the largest financial return. The largest behavioural return: the change in the felt experience of financial life that is produced by having a genuine buffer between your income and the unexpected.

A household without an emergency reserve experiences every unexpected expense as a financial emergency. The car repair, the medical bill, the appliance failure, the period of reduced income: each of these becomes a crisis that activates the threat response, requires anxiety-driven decision-making, and often results in the kind of expensive debt that perpetuates the cycle. The financial position, which was managing, suddenly becomes a problem.

A household with three months of essential expenses in a named, separate reserve account experiences the same unexpected expense as an inconvenience. It is absorbed by the reserve, the reserve is replenished over the following months, and the rest of the financial structure, including the investment automation, continues undisturbed. The experience of that resilience, the first time a genuine emergency is handled without a crisis, is one of the most powerful pieces of financial evidence a nervous system can accumulate.

The initial target should not be three months of expenses. Three months is the right long-term target, but as an initial goal it is often large enough to feel unachievable alongside debt clearance and investment contributions. The useful initial target is smaller: whatever amount would cover the single most likely financial surprise in your specific life. For most households, this is somewhere between one and three thousand in currencyneutral terms, enough for a car repair or an appliance replacement or an unexpected medical co-payment. That amount is achievable in most budgets within two to three months of consistent automated saving.

Name the account. The specific label, Emergency Reserve, is not incidental. Mental accounting, the psychological tendency to treat money differently depending on the category it has been assigned to, means that a named reserve with an explicit purpose is significantly less likely to be raided for nonemergency purposes than a generic savings account. The name is the barrier. Keep the barrier.

Move Five: The Annual Strategic Review

The five moves are listed in a specific sequence because sequence matters. The Complete Financial Picture must precede everything else, because every subsequent decision depends on knowing your starting position clearly. The Automation Foundation follows, because removing recurring decisions from the domain of active choice creates the stable base that everything else is built on. The Debt Sequence runs in parallel with automation once the foundation is established. The Emergency Reserve is built simultaneously with debt clearance, starting small. The Annual Strategic Review begins after the first full year of practice.

Do not try to implement all five simultaneously. The attempt to change everything at once is itself a form of the Preparation Infinity pattern: ambitious in the moment of high motivation, unsustainable when motivation normalizes. One layer at a time. Stabilized before the next. That is what lasts.

Everything described in Chapters Ten through Twelve operates at the level of weekly and monthly practice. The Annual Strategic Review operates at a different level: trajectory. Once a year, on a date set and held consistently, you step back from the operational detail and examine the direction of travel.

The structure takes two to three hours done properly. First: compare your current net worth to last year's figure. Second: review the Opportunity Audit from Chapter Four and assess how each area has changed. Third: review the automation architecture and consider whether contribution levels should be adjusted given changes in income. Fourth: identify three to five specific financial improvements for the coming year, each with a planned implementation date.

The Annual Strategic Review is where strategy lives. The Weekly Financial Review is where consistency lives. Both are necessary, and neither is sufficient alone. The consistent practice without periodic strategic review drifts from the most important opportunities. The strategic review without consistent practice produces plans that are not implemented. Together, they constitute the complete architecture of a financial life that is both well-managed and well-directed.

3.4 Investing Without the Dread

What markets actually are, and how to participate without being controlled by them

"The stock market is a device for transferring money from the impatient to the patient"

- *Warren Buffett*

In the autumn of 2008, at the worst point of the global financial crisis, Peter Lynch gave an interview that most of the financial media ignored.

Lynch, who had managed the Fidelity Magellan Fund from 1977 to 1990 and turned it into the best-performing mutual fund in the world during that period, was asked what ordinary investors should do given the market conditions. His answer was characteristically direct: know what you own and why you own it, and if neither of those things has changed, do not let the price change your behaviour.

What Lynch was describing was not indifference to the market's movements. He was describing the specific cognitive discipline that separates the long-term investor, who builds wealth, from the short-term reactor, who consistently buys high and sells low. The discipline is not complicated. It is also not natural, because it requires the human nervous system to behave in ways that are contrary to several of its most deeply encoded instincts.

This chapter is about building that discipline. Not through willpower or the suppression of the anxiety that market volatility produces, which is both impossible and unnecessary, but through understanding markets accurately enough that the anxiety loses its power to drive behaviour in the direction that costs the most.

What the Market Actually Is

Most financial anxiety about investing is rooted in an inaccurate understanding of what the market actually is. People understand it, vaguely, as a kind of large casino where prices move unpredictably and the house eventually wins. Or as a competition between informed professionals and naive amateurs, in which the amateurs are reliably exploited. Or as a mechanism whose primary feature is the risk of losing everything.

None of these descriptions is accurate, and the inaccuracy matters because it produces financial behaviour that is poorly suited to the actual environment.

The market, in its most fundamental form, is a mechanism by which ordinary people can own fractional stakes in real businesses. When you invest in a broad market index fund, you are becoming a part-owner, a tiny but genuine part-owner, of the companies in that index: the businesses that produce the goods people buy, provide the services people use, employ the people who build the economy. These businesses are run by large teams of motivated people trying to grow them. They generate revenues. They pay employees. They invest in their own futures. They produce, over time, profits that flow to their owners.

The price of your investment in these businesses fluctuates daily, hourly, and sometimes dramatically. That fluctuation reflects the collective assessment of millions of market participants about what those businesses are worth at any given moment, and that collective assessment is frequently wrong in the short term, driven by fear and greed and momentum and news events that turn out to be less significant than they appeared. In the long run, the assessment tends to converge on something closer to the underlying reality: the actual value generated by actual businesses employing actual people.

Understanding this changes the emotional experience of market volatility. A ten percent fall in the market is not, for the long-term investor, ten percent of their wealth disappearing. It is the same fractional ownership of the same businesses, temporarily priced ten percent lower by a market that is currently more fearful than usual. The businesses have not changed. The price has. And price, for the patient investor with no immediate need to sell, is largely noise.

The 2008 Lesson, Fully Told

In September 2008, Lehman Brothers collapsed. Over the following six weeks, the United States equity market fell approximately forty percent from its recent peak. The declines were not gradual. There were days when the market fell five, six, seven percent in a single session. Financial commentators used words like unprecedented, catastrophic, systemic. The atmosphere was genuinely frightening, and not irrationally so.

What happened to investors in the months that followed depended almost entirely on what they did during those six weeks of peak panic.

Investors who sold, locking in losses at or near the bottom of the decline, experienced those losses as permanent. Many of them did not re-enter the market until well after the recovery, because the same anxiety that drove the selling also prevented the buying. They sold low and, when they eventually returned, bought higher. The mathematical outcome of that sequence, played out across millions of individual accounts, was a real and lasting reduction in retirement wealth that had nothing to do with the underlying performance of the businesses in their portfolios.

Investors who held, and investors who continued their automated monthly contributions through the decline, experienced a different sequence. Their account values fell with the market. Then, as the market recovered through 2009 and 2010, their account values recovered.

Those who had continued contributing through the decline had been buying units at the lowest prices available, which meant the recovery lifted those units disproportionately. By 2013, the major indices had not only recovered but exceeded their 2007 peaks. By 2019, they had roughly tripled from the 2009 lows.

The investors who held and continued contributing did not do so because they were smarter than those who sold. In most cases, they did so because they had built the specific infrastructure that made holding the default rather than a recurring active choice. Automated contributions. Infrequent account reviews.

A written investment policy that specified what conditions would and would not constitute reasons to change strategy. These were not indicators of superior analytical ability. They were the outputs of a system designed to protect the investor from their own nervous system at its worst moments.

That is the practical lesson of 2008 for the ordinary investor: not that markets always recover, which is a statement about the past rather than a guarantee about the future, but that the investors who do best are those who have built systems that make patient behaviour the path of least resistance rather than the path of maximum willpower.

The Only Investment Discipline That Matters

If there is one sentence this chapter is designed to produce in the reader, it is this: for the long-term investor in diversified index funds, staying invested through volatility is the primary investment discipline. Not stock selection, not market timing, not active management, not rebalancing frequency. Staying in.

This is an unusual claim for a chapter about investing to make, because it locates the most important investment skill entirely outside the domain of financial analysis. It suggests that the most consequential thing most investors can do is not become better at evaluating securities but become better at managing their own nervous system's response to price movements.

The evidence for this claim is extensive and consistent. Research on investor returns consistently finds that the average investor earns significantly less than the average fund, not because the funds perform poorly but because investors buy and sell at the wrong moments. They buy after strong performance, when prices are high. They sell during poor performance, when prices are low. The gap between the fund's return and the investor's return is driven almost entirely by timing: the human tendency to buy enthusiasm and sell fear.

The remedy is structural. Automated monthly contributions ensure that the investment happens regardless of market conditions, at high prices and low prices, averaging the cost over time. Infrequent review, quarterly for most long-term investors, reduces the number of moments at which the anxious nervous system can generate a sell decision. A written investment policy, agreed in a calm moment and consulted during volatile ones, provides an external reference point that is not subject to the cortisol-driven distortion of the moment.

Starting: The Most Imperfect Decision That Still Works

The investment conversation often gets stuck at the question of where to begin: which fund, which platform, which allocation, which rebalancing strategy. This is Preparation Infinity in one of its most socially acceptable forms. The research has the appearance of diligence. The delay has the cost of foregone compounding.

For the first investment, the details matter significantly less than the fact. A broad market index fund, one that tracks a wide range of companies across the economy, is an entirely appropriate starting point for most new investors in most markets. The expense ratio of the fund matters over decades; it matters considerably less than whether you are invested at all. The allocation between domestic and international equities matters; it matters less than whether the practice of regular investing has been established.

Open the account. Start the contribution. Automate it. Then leave it alone for twelve months and experience what twelve months of market participation actually feels like: some months up, some months down, the overall trajectory determined by factors entirely outside your control, the contribution arriving faithfully each month regardless. After twelve months of that experience, you will have information that no amount of prior research could have provided: you will know how you actually respond to volatility, which positions in your portfolio feel comfortable and which feel uncomfortable, and what refinements, if any, are warranted. You cannot know these things before you have the experience. No amount of research substitutes for it. The refinements are real questions worth addressing eventually. They are not the reason the account has not been opened. Open the account. Start the contribution.

The refinements can come once you have twelve months of actual investment experience to inform them, experience that no amount of prior research can substitute for.

A broadly diversified equity index fund tracking a major market index is an appropriate starting point for most investors. Its expense ratio will be low. Its diversification will be high. Its performance over long periods will approximate the return of the market itself. That return, held consistently and reinvested automatically over a working life, is what builds the outcomes this book has been describing throughout.

The most common version of Preparation Infinity in investing is the search for the right fund. Research into expense ratios, fund manager track records, factor exposures, and regional allocations is genuine and the differences between funds are real over long periods. It is also true that for an investor who currently holds nothing, the difference between a good fund and an excellent fund is a rounding error compared to the difference between being invested and being uninvested.

On Finding the Right Fund

This is the mathematical expression of the holding discipline. Dollar-cost averaging makes staying invested the structural default rather than a monthly act of courage. It is one of the most powerful financial tools available to any investor, and it requires no market knowledge whatsoever to use. The only skill required is maintaining the automation, which means not cancelling the transfer when the market falls. The threebreath reset from Chapter Six is the tool for that specific moment.

The 2008 market decline illustrates this with unusual clarity. An investor who maintained a fixed monthly contribution through the eighteen months of the decline was buying units at progressively lower prices throughout. When the recovery came, those units recovered in value. The investor who stopped contributing because the market felt dangerous forfeited both the lower-priced units they would have bought during the worst of the decline and the disproportionate recovery those units would have delivered. Same market. Entirely different financial outcome. The difference was automation.

When you invest a fixed amount every month through an automated contribution, you are doing something with a technical name that sounds sophisticated and a mechanism that is entirely simple: dollar-cost averaging. In months when the market is high, your fixed contribution buys fewer units. In months when the market is low, it buys more. Over time, this natural variation means you accumulate more units at lower prices than at higher prices. You are not timing the market, which is impossible to do reliably. You are averaging into it, which requires no prediction and no decision.

Dollar-Cost Averaging: Why Automation Is the Strategy

One final note on the emotional quality of long-term investing that is almost never mentioned but is worth saying clearly: it is boring. Boring by design. The long-term index investor's experience is watching a number go up and down without being able to predict its direction, for years at a time, trusting a process whose most significant results are decades away. This is not a failure of the strategy. It is the strategy. The return available to the patient investor is, in substantial part, the return available to whoever can tolerate the tedium and the uncertainty long enough to collect it. Boring, maintained consistently over a working life, is what Ronald Read built an eight-million-dollar estate with.

Boring, sustained for a working life, is what built Ronald Read's eight-million-dollar estate. The investment that runs quietly in the background while you live your life is the investment that compounds most powerfully. Chapter Fourteen addresses the income that feeds it.

3.5 Earn What You Are Worth

The compensation conversation most people avoid and exactly what it costs them

"Ask for what you want and be prepared to get it"

\- *Maya Angelou*

Of all the financial opportunities available to most working professionals, the salary negotiation produces the largest return per hour invested and is the most consistently avoided.

The mathematics of this are straightforward and worth stating precisely before we discuss the psychology, because the psychology is considerably more tractable when you have looked clearly at what the avoidance is costing.

The compensation gap, the difference between your current salary and the market rate for your role, experience, and location, does not stay constant from year to year. It compounds. If you are currently paid ten percent below market rate and you remain at your current employer for five years with market-rate annual increases applied to a below-market base, you end those five years further below market than when you started. Every raise, calculated as a percentage of the current base, is a percentage of the lower number. Every job offer you consider during that period is benchmarked against the lower number. The gap grows unless specific action is taken to close it.

Research by economists at Carnegie Mellon and elsewhere has estimated that professionals who negotiate consistently, at every job change and every performance review, earn substantially more over a thirty-year career than those who accept what is offered.

The figure varies by study, industry, and geography, but the direction is always the same and the magnitude is always larger than most people expect before they calculate it.

The chapter is not primarily about the mathematics. The mathematics are available to anyone who runs the calculation. The chapter is about why the calculation does not produce the conversation, and what actually does.

A Scene From My Own Career

A few years into my career, when I was working in a regional role and had been performing well by most measurable standards, I spent approximately four months preparing for a salary conversation that I never had.

I researched my market rate. I documented my contributions. I rehearsed the conversation in my head, in the shower, on market visits, in the car between meetings, with enough repetition that I could have delivered it in my sleep. I knew what I was going to say, what the likely responses were, and how I would handle each one. I was, by any technical measure, more prepared for that conversation than for most professional presentations I have given.

What I could not seem to do was schedule it.

The reasons were always plausible. The quarter was ending and it was a difficult moment. My manager was under pressure and it was not the right time. The company was going through a reorganisation and the dust had not settled. I should wait until the next review cycle when there would be a more formal mechanism. Each reason made sense on its own. Together, they constituted four months of elaborate, energetic avoidance.

What I eventually understood, once the conversation finally happened and went considerably better than the four months of dread had suggested it would, was that the preparation had been both genuine and a form of protection. Preparation requires no vulnerability. Preparation can go on indefinitely. The conversation requires commitment and the possibility of a no, and no, in the context of a salary discussion, can feel like a verdict on your worth rather than a response to a request in a specific budget cycle.

The no, when it eventually came in a modified form, was not a verdict. It was information. Specific information about timing and budget and what would be required for the conversation to produce a different result in the next cycle. Acting on that 184 information produced a different result six months later. The four months of preparation produced nothing except a modest improvement in my ability to rehearse conversations I was not having.

Why the Conversation Feels Different

In my years managing commercial teams, I watched consistently capable negotiators become hesitant and overqualified when the subject was their own compensation. The same person who could construct a mutually beneficial commercial arrangement with a difficult client could not ask their own manager for an increase without several layers of apology and qualification.

The difference is not one of skill. It is one of emotional stakes. Commercial negotiation is external: you represent an organisation's interests in a context where the relationship is professional and the potential rejection is operational. Salary negotiation is internal: you assert a claim about your own worth in a context where the relationship is personal and the potential rejection feels like a judgment about you.

This distinction matters because it explains why more information about negotiation tactics is rarely the primary intervention required. The person who has researched salary negotiation techniques extensively and still has not had the conversation does not lack tactics. They lack the specific physiological regulation capacity to enter the conversation while their nervous system is signaling maximum threat.

The three-breath reset from Chapter Six, applied immediately before the conversation begins, changes the biochemical conditions of the first thirty seconds in a way that information about negotiation tactics does not. The body scan that identifies where the tension is sitting gives you something concrete to regulate rather than an abstract anxiety to overcome. These are not soft practices. They are the specific interventions that make the technical preparation usable.

The Preparation That Changes the Outcome

With the physiological foundation in place, the preparation for the compensation conversation has three components. Each is important. The third is the one most people skip.

Start the practice now, even if the next review is months away. Open a document and write three specific contributions from the last ninety days. Three concrete, evidenced outcomes with measurable results. Check one salary benchmarking source and write down the median and 75th percentile for your profile. Write a specific number at the top of the page. The preparation starts today. The conversation happens when the calendar is ready. The outcome is influenced significantly by how long and how consistently the preparation has been running before that conversation begins.

This approach changes the experience of the conversation from an emotionally loaded singular event into the professional presentation of regularly maintained evidence. The emotional charge reduces when the preparation is continuous rather than crisis-driven, when the evidence is specific rather than impressionistic, and when the number has been decided and practised rather than produced under pressure.

The preparation framework described in this chapter works best when it is maintained continuously rather than assembled under pressure in the weeks before a review cycle. The professional who keeps a running document of their specific contributions and outcomes throughout the year, updated monthly, arrives at each review cycle with the documentation already done. The market rate research is refreshed annually as part of the Annual Strategic

Review. The specific number is prepared and rehearsed in advance rather than generated in the room.

Building the Practice, Not Just the Conversation

Research on long-term earnings consistently shows that professionals who negotiate at every opportunity earn between thirty and fifty percent more over a thirty-year career than those who accept what is offered. The precise figure varies by profession and context. The direction is consistent and the magnitude is consistently larger than most people estimate before they run the numbers. This is the investment framing of the salary conversation: the discomfort is the cost, and the return compounds for decades.

A professional earning eighty thousand per year in their currency who is five percent below market rate gains four thousand per year from a successful negotiation to market rate. But that four thousand is not the end of the story. The following year's increase is calculated from eighty-four thousand rather than eighty thousand. The bonus is a percentage of eighty-four thousand. The next job offer is benchmarked against eighty-four thousand. The gap between the negotiated and the unnegotiated path widens every year, compounding in the same direction as investment returns, for the remainder of the working life.

Most people calculate the benefit of a salary negotiation as the immediate annual increase. This calculation significantly underestimates the actual financial impact because it ignores what happens to every subsequent number that uses the current salary as its baseline.

The Compounding Effect of One Successful Conversation

The first component is market research: an honest, specific, multi-source assessment of what the market pays for your role, your experience level, and your geography. Not a single data point from one job board. At least three independent sources: professional network salary tools, industry-specific salary surveys, and a brief conversation with a recruiter who operates in your sector. From these, establish the median and the 75th percentile. These are your reference points, not your aspirational ceiling.

The second component is contribution documentation: a written record of what you have specifically delivered in your current role over the relevant review period. Not a description of your responsibilities, which is what you were hired to do. Specific outputs: the project completed under budget, the target exceeded by a measurable margin, the problem solved that had been unresolved, the relationship built that opened a commercial opportunity. The documentation should be concrete enough that someone unfamiliar with your day-to-day work could read it and understand exactly what you contributed. Vague claims about working hard are easy to dismiss. Specific evidence of output is difficult to dismiss.

The third component, the one most often skipped, is a specific number. Not a range. A number. Research consistently shows that anchoring the conversation with a specific ask produces better outcomes than expressing a range, because a range implicitly invites the respondent to consider the lower end as the reasonable midpoint of their counter. The number should be at or near the 75th percentile of your market research, on the basis that your specific contributions and performance position you toward the upper end of the market. Ask for it without apology or qualification. State the figure. Then stop talking. The silence after the figure is uncomfortable and important. It is not your job to fill it.

The silence is the space in which the other person processes what they have heard and formulates their response. Filling it with qualifications, such as 'I know the timing might not be ideal' or 'I understand if that's not possible right now', is a negotiation with yourself that concedes ground before the other person has had a chance to respond.

What Happens When the Answer Is No

A no in a salary conversation is almost never a final verdict. It is almost always specific information about what would need to change for the answer to become yes. Getting that specific information, by asking directly and without defensiveness what conditions would need to be different, converts a closed door into a set of directions.

The most useful follow-up question after a no is: what would I need to deliver or demonstrate in the next six months for this conversation to have a different outcome? That question accomplishes several things simultaneously. It signals that you are not withdrawing from the professional relationship in response to the no. It creates a specific, agreed-upon set of criteria that can be worked toward and referenced in the next conversation. And it gives the manager something specific to say to their own leadership, which makes the subsequent yes considerably easier to obtain.

If the no is a definitive one with no path forward despite an evidenced case at market rate, that is also information: about whether the current role is the best available use of your professional capacity. The compensation conversation, in that version, is the beginning of a different kind of planning rather than the end of the conversation.

Something I observed consistently across the years I spent managing people deserves a direct statement consistently across the years I spent managing people, because it is the thing most people most underestimate before they have the conversation.

The professionals who asked for what they believed they were worth, directly and with evidence and without extended apology, were without exception more respected for having asked than they feared they would be. Not always paid more immediately. Always respected more. The ask, professionally made, signals a self-assessment that managers find useful regardless of whether the immediate budget accommodates it.

The salary conversation, professionally made, always produces more than the fear before it suggested it would. Sometimes more money. Always more respect. Chapter Fifteen addresses the structural risk that sits underneath any single income source.

3.6 Building Income Resilience

Why one income stream is a structural risk, and how to reduce it

"Do not put all your eggs in one basket"

- *Common wisdom, consistently undervalued*

One specific financial vulnerability is invisible in normal conditions that is invisible in normal conditions and becomes dramatically visible in abnormal ones.

It is not the vulnerability of poor investment choices or excessive debt, which produce visible evidence of distress over time. It is the vulnerability of complete dependence on a single income source: the situation in which your entire financial life rests on one employer's continued decision to pay you at the current level.

Most professional households are in this situation and most of them do not think about it as a structural risk because it has not yet been triggered. The income arrives each month. The bills are paid. The savings account grows, or approximately grows, or means to grow. The arrangement seems fine. Then something happens that is not fine, a redundancy, an illness, an organisational restructuring, a market contraction, and the arrangement that seemed fine reveals itself as a single point of failure that has just failed.

This chapter is not primarily about investing or savings. It is about the distribution of risk: the practical steps available to most professionals for building at least some income diversity, even if what that diversity initially amounts to is modest, so that the financial life does not rest entirely on a single decision by a single employer.

What Income Resilience Actually Means

Income resilience does not mean having multiple full-time jobs. It does not mean quitting the salaried career to become an entrepreneur. It means having at least one income stream, even a small one, that is not entirely dependent on your current employer's continued presence in your life.

The value of a second income stream is not primarily in its initial size. A modest additional income of five hundred a month in a currency-neutral sense does not transform the financial position in the immediate term. What it does is change the character of the financial position: from a position in which everything depends on one source to a position in which two sources contribute. That change in character has value that exceeds its financial magnitude, because it changes the experience of the primary income source from the only thing standing between you and financial difficulty to one of two things providing financial stability.

Holding that understanding changes the felt experience of the monthly transfer. It is not deferred gratification. It is construction. Each month, the structure becomes slightly more sound. The single-income vulnerability is slightly reduced. The eventual position of having investment income that supplements or could partially replace earned income is closer than it was the previous month. That perspective, held consistently, is among the most useful things in this book for sustaining the investment practice through the periods when its payoff feels far away.

A portfolio generating a four percent annual distribution, which is a reasonable long-run expectation for a balanced investment portfolio, produces a meaningful monthly income at a scale that is achievable through consistent investment over a twenty-year working life for a professional who has been investing even modest monthly amounts. The specific figure depends on starting age, contribution level, and return outcomes over the period. What is significant is that the investment practice already in place is building toward this form of income resilience as a natural consequence. The monthly contribution is not only providing retirement security. It is incrementally reducing the degree of dependence on any single employer's continued presence in your life.

Asset income, earnings generated by what you own rather than by time you spend, is the most durable form of income resilience and the eventual destination of the investment practice described in Chapter Thirteen. Understanding what that destination looks like in practical terms gives the monthly contribution a specificity that abstract compounding often does not.

Where the Investment Practice Is Building Toward

The first client, or the first paying reader, or the first student in a course you have designed, is the evidence that the value transfers outside the institutional context. That first piece of evidence is disproportionately important, not for its financial magnitude but for what it changes in the nervous system's prediction about your independent professional worth. One client changes the prediction. The subsequent clients build on a foundation the first client established.

The answer is that the institutional context is not what creates the value. It is the arrangement through which currently, the value is being exchanged. Your expertise, your network, your specific professional knowledge, these are yours. They exist independently of any particular employer's decision to pay for them. The employer has been the distribution mechanism for that value. A second income stream is a second distribution mechanism for the same underlying value.

Building additional income requires confronting a psychological obstacle that is different from the financial anxiety discussed elsewhere in this book. It is not primarily anxiety. It is identity. For most salaried professionals, professional identity is deeply tied to the institutional context in which the salary is earned. The idea of independently offering value outside that institutional structure, as a consultant, a teacher, a writer, can feel presumptuous. Who am I to charge for this outside the company that pays me for it?

The Identity Obstacle

There is also an optionality dimension. The professional who has developed a secondary income stream over two or three years, however modest, has developed capabilities, reputation, and relationships outside their current employer that increase their options in ways that the financial income alone does not capture. They have demonstrated, to themselves and to a market, that their skills have value independent of the specific institutional context in which those skills are currently deployed. That demonstration changes how they negotiate with their current employer, because the negotiation is no longer happening from a position of complete dependence.

The Colleague Who Left

During a period of organisational restructuring at one of the companies I worked for, a colleague of mine, a genuinely capable professional with a strong track record and solid relationships across the organisation, was made redundant. The decision was not performance-related. He was caught in a restructuring that eliminated an entire function, and his particular role was one of the ones eliminated.

What followed was a sequence I have thought about many times since. He had been earning well for several years. He was highly regarded professionally. He had every reasonable expectation of being able to find a comparable role within a reasonable period. All of this was true. What was also true was that he had no financial buffer of any significance, no secondary income of any kind, and no professional presence outside the company he had just left. His entire professional and financial identity was housed within a single institution that had just asked him to leave.

The urgency of his financial situation, which became acute within about six weeks of the redundancy, compressed his options significantly. He took a role that was below his capabilities and below his previous compensation because the financial pressure left him no room to be patient. The role set a new lower benchmark for subsequent compensation conversations. The compressed options produced a compressed outcome.

I am not describing this to suggest he had done something wrong. His choices had been entirely normal. Most professionals make the same choices. What I took from watching his situation was a clear illustration of something that is easy to understand abstractly and difficult to feel urgently before it becomes relevant: complete income dependence is a structural vulnerability, and the time to address structural vulnerabilities is before they are triggered, not after.

The Accessible Forms of Additional Income

The most accessible form of additional income for most professionals is what might be called knowledge monetisation: earning income from what you already know, in a form that is separate from your current employer.

Consulting or freelancing in your professional domain is the most direct version. If you have spent ten years developing expertise in a specific area, that expertise has value to people and organisations who need it and do not have it. The initial clients are almost always in your existing professional network, which makes the starting conditions more accessible than building a client base from scratch. The initial projects are almost always small, which makes the starting time commitment manageable. The income is almost always modest in the first year, which makes it poor as a replacement for a primary salary and excellent as a beginning of income diversification.

Writing in your professional domain is another form. Not necessarily a book, though that is one option, as you are demonstrating with the project this book represents. Articles, online content, professional commentary in forums and networks relevant to your field. These forms of content creation build professional reputation over time as a secondary benefit alongside whatever income they eventually produce. They also establish a professional presence outside your current employer that has value independent of the income it generates.

Teaching or training in your area of expertise is a third form. Workshops, online courses, mentoring, speaking at professional events. These paths leverage the same knowledge base as consulting but tend to produce more scalable income because the same content can reach multiple people simultaneously.

The fourth form, and the one with the longest horizon but the most durable eventual outcome, is asset income: investment dividends, rental income, or any other form of income generated by assets you own rather than by time you spend. This form of income is the furthest from immediate accessibility for most professionals at the beginning of their wealth-building journey, but it is the destination that the investment practice in Chapter Thirteen is building toward over years and decades.

The One-Hour-Per-Week Principle

The most common objection to building additional income, and the one I take most seriously because it is often genuinely true, is that there is no time. The professional working full time, managing family responsibilities, and trying to maintain some semblance of physical and mental health does not have unlimited discretionary hours.

The one-hour-per-week principle is designed for exactly that reality. Not ten hours per week, which is not available to most people in full-time professional roles without meaningful sacrifice in other areas. Not a dramatic restructuring of priorities. One deliberate hour per week, protected from other claims, directed toward whatever form of additional income development is most relevant to your specific situation.

One hour per week is fifty-two hours per year. Fifty-two hours of deliberate, directed effort on a specific professional capability or business development project is not nothing. Over a year, fifty-two hours of writing produces a substantial body of work. Fifty-two hours of consulting outreach produces a small client list and several projects. Fifty-two hours of course development produces a publishable course. These are not transformative outcomes in a single year. They are the beginning of something that compounds, as everything in this book compounds, through consistent application over time.

Start with identifying the one form of additional income most accessible to your specific skills and network. Then protect one hour per week for it. Not aspirationally. Actually: in the calendar, defended against other claims, used for the specific purpose for which it was protected. Do that for twelve months before evaluating whether it is worth extending or adjusting. Twelve months of one protected hour per week produces enough evidence to evaluate. Twelve months of intermittent intention produces nothing except the continued vulnerability of the single-income structure.

Part 4

BUILD WEALTH FOR LIFE

Sustaining financial momentum through the full complexity of a real life

4.1 When the Fear Comes Back

Resilience, relapse, and the practice of returning

"Fall seven times. Stand up eight."

- *Japanese proverb*

The third is your return step: the one specific action you will take to resume the practice after any period of disruption. One account opened. One journal entry written. One breath before looking at the numbers. Specified in advance and written down, this step is available without deliberation at the moment you decide to return. Write the protocol now. Put it somewhere you will find it if you need it.

The second is your list of protected automations: the specific financial practices that continue regardless of the disruption. Your floor. For most people, this includes the automated investment contribution unless the disruption is severe enough to require suspension, the emergency reserve maintenance, and the weekly review even if briefer than usual.

Your protocol has three components. The first is your regulation sequence: the specific physiological tools you will use in the first hours of a financial shock, in the specific order you have found effective. Three-breath reset, then body scan, then a phone call to a specific trusted person who provides perspective rather than panic.

The most useful action this chapter asks of you is to write your personal resilience protocol before any disruption arrives. The quality of the decisions you make during a financial shock depends significantly on whether you are drawing on a pre-built protocol or constructing one under duress.

Write Your Resilience Protocol Before You Need It

He did not sell. The market recovered within eight months. The contributions made during the decline bought units at the lowest prices of the decade. His portfolio two years later was substantially higher than it had been before the correction began. The practical intervention that changed the outcome was not financial analysis. It was the physiological regulation practice from Chapter Six, applied to a specific moment of acute anxiety by someone who had built enough of the Clarity Foundation to use them. The practices worked because they changed the conditions under which the decision was made.

What he was experiencing was not a rational assessment. He was experiencing the cortisol spike of watching a large number decrease rapidly, processed through a nervous system that was interpreting the decrease as a threat and generating an urgent impulse to stop it. We talked through the twenty-fourhour hold. We talked about the difference between the paper value of the portfolio, which had declined, and the number of units he owned, which had not changed. We talked about what the automated contribution would buy the following week at the lower unit prices.

The market had declined roughly twenty percent over six weeks. His portfolio, built over nearly a decade, had fallen in paper value by an amount that felt physically significant when he looked at the account screen. He was not in financial difficulty. He did not need the money. His investment horizon was more than fifteen years. By every rational measure, the correct action was to do nothing and let the automated contribution continue.

A few years ago, during a period of significant market volatility, a member of my extended professional network sent me a message that read: I am about to sell everything. Talk me out of it.

A Real Moment of Disruption

Let me begin this chapter with something that most books about financial behaviour change do not say, because it sits awkwardly alongside the implicit promise that the right approach will solve the problem.

The anxiety you have been working with throughout this book is not going to disappear permanently. It will diminish with practice. It will become more manageable, more recognisable, and less capable of driving your behaviour without your awareness. The practices in Part Three will genuinely change your relationship with financial engagement. What they will not do is make you immune to difficulty.

Life provides recurring occasions for the old patterns to reassert themselves. A significant financial shock, a period of prolonged stress at work, a relationship change, a health event, a market downturn severe enough to make the investment account uncomfortable to look at: any of these can temporarily reactivate the threat response at its previous intensity, regardless of how much progress has been made. Expecting otherwise is not optimism. It is a setup for the particular despair of believing that the return of anxiety means the work has failed.

The work has not failed. The return of difficulty is not failure. It is the normal texture of any practice maintained through a real life. The measure of success is not the permanent absence of the old patterns. It is your relationship with them when they return: how quickly you recognise them, how effectively you regulate the physiological response, and how soon you return to productive financial engagement after a period of disruption.

The Twenty-Four-Hour Hold

When a significant financial disruption arrives, a redundancy, a large unexpected expense, a market decline that makes the investment account uncomfortable to look at, a change in household income for any reason, the single most important thing to know is this: the financial decisions you make in the first twenty-four hours after the disruption will almost certainly be worse than the decisions you make a week later.

This is not a counsel of paralysis. Some financial situations require immediate action. A missed payment that will attract a penalty tomorrow requires attention today. An expiring insurance policy requires renewal before it lapses. Timesensitive matters must be addressed on their timescale.

Strategic financial decisions do not need to be made in the first twenty-four hours. How to restructure the approach in response to a job loss. Whether to change the investment allocation in response to a market decline. How to reorganise the budget in response to reduced income. These decisions, made during the acute cortisol spike of the initial shock, are made by the compromised version of the prefrontal cortex. A day of regulation, of conversation with someone trusted, of allowing the initial physiological response to de-escalate, produces better decisions than the same decisions made in the first hour of maximum anxiety.

I call this the twenty-four-hour hold, and I have found it to be one of the most practically useful concepts in this book for the moments when it is actually needed. The hold is not passivity. During the hold, you are doing the physiological regulation work from Chapter Six. You are talking to someone who knows you and can provide perspective rather than panic. You are allowing the cortisol to drop far enough that the subsequent thinking has meaningful prefrontal cortex participation. Then you make the decisions.

Protecting What Has Been Built

One of the more counterintuitive pieces of financial guidance I can offer is about the period of disruption specifically: the financial practices you have built are most valuable precisely when maintaining them is most difficult.

The instinct during financial difficulty is to suspend the automated investment, because the money feels needed elsewhere. This instinct is sometimes correct: if the disruption is severe enough that the investment contribution represents money required for essential expenses, pausing it is appropriate and this is exactly what the emergency reserve was built to prevent from being necessary.

More often, the instinct fires in situations where the contribution could continue without genuine hardship, but where the psychological experience of the disruption makes the contribution feel vulnerable. The automated investment running during a period when money feels tight produces a slight anxiety each month when it transfers. That anxiety is manageable. Suspending the investment converts a slight monthly anxiety into a signal to the nervous system that the financial foundation is not stable, that what has been built is conditional on good conditions, that the practice is only for easy periods.

This signal is expensive. Not because of the missed contribution alone, though that has a cost. Because of what it teaches the nervous system about the practice: that it does not hold under pressure. And practices that do not hold under pressure are not practices. They are good intentions with a specific failure condition.

The emergency reserve was built, in Chapter Twelve, for this exact moment. Its specific purpose is to handle the unexpected expenses and the periods of reduced income that would otherwise require raiding the investment contributions or accumulating expensive debt. If the reserve is there and sufficient for the disruption, the investment practice continues. If the reserve has been exhausted, the investment pauses until the reserve is rebuilt. That is the intended sequence. It protects the practice during exactly the conditions that would otherwise undermine it.

On Relapse: The Most Honest Section of This Book

There will be periods when the practice you have built stops. The weekly review does not happen for a month. The anxiety about a specific financial situation returns at its previous intensity and you find yourself avoiding the accounts in the old way. The automated contributions run, because they require no decision to maintain, but nothing else does, and the quiet maintenance of the automation becomes a substitute for the fuller engagement the practice was supposed to represent.

This is not failure. This is the entirely normal pattern of any behavioural practice maintained through the complexity of a real life. Every meaningful behavioural change, in every domain, is characterised by periods of consistent progress followed by periods of disruption and partial regression, followed by recovery and resumption. The people who make the most durable long-term changes are not those who never experience these disruptions. They are those who return most quickly after them.

What makes return easier is removing the requirement that it be a full return. The person who has been away from the practice for three weeks does not need to restart with the complete weekly review and the full evidence journal and the three-breath reset and the body scan and all the automations checked. They need one step. One account opened. One entry written in the journal. One breath taken before looking at a balance. One step, taken today rather than when circumstances are more suitable.

The practice, once established, does not need to be rebuilt from the beginning each time it is disrupted. It needs to be resumed, from wherever you actually are, with the understanding that resumption is the thing and the size of the resuming step is secondary. The journal entry that says 'I have 207 not done this for three weeks, I am doing it now, the balance is what it is' is worth more than the journal entry that was going to be comprehensive and perfect and was never written.

The Long View, Held Lightly

The definition of enough that serves you is an internal one: what specific conditions, described in concrete felt terms, would produce the experience of security and freedom you are working toward? That definition does not move when a colleague is promoted or a social media contact posts photographs from an expensive trip. It remains constant as a reference point for your own trajectory, and it makes the financial practice immune to the comparison noise that derails many otherwise sound approaches to wealth building.

Financial comparison is also almost universally inaccurate. What most people display about their financial lives is a curated surface that bears a complex relationship to the underlying reality. The visible signals of financial abundance, the cars, the holidays, the home renovations, are often financed by debt or by the sacrifice of less visible forms of financial security. The household whose life looks financially abundant may be carrying significant consumer debt. The household whose life looks modest may be quietly building something durable. Comparison based on what is visible is comparison to a fiction.

One of the most reliable ways to make enough impossible to achieve is to define it in relative rather than absolute terms. The person who defines enough as having more than their peers has created a target that moves every time their comparison group moves. This is the money status script from Chapter Seven in its most practically self-defeating form.

The Comparison Problem

This is not an argument against building wealth. It is an argument for building toward something specific and felt rather than toward maximum accumulation as an abstract end. The person who has defined their specific version of enough and who is building deliberately toward it is building toward an actual felt experience rather than a number that recedes as it is approached. The wealth practice is the mechanism. The felt experience of security and freedom is the destination.

A subsequent large-scale study by Matthew Killingsworth found a more continuous relationship, suggesting the plateau varies significantly by individual and circumstance. Both studies agree on one point that is directly relevant here: the largest wellbeing gain from income occurs in the lower range, the move from genuine financial precarity to basic security. Above a threshold of comfortable sufficiency, the additional wellbeing return from additional income diminishes considerably for most people.

The relationship between income and wellbeing has been studied extensively, and the findings are more nuanced than the popular summary suggests. Daniel Kahneman and Angus Deaton's influential 2010 study found that emotional wellbeing, the felt quality of daily experience, increased with income up to a threshold representing comfortable sufficiency and then levelled off. Cognitive life satisfaction, how people evaluated their lives when asked to reflect, continued to improve with income above that threshold, but the day-to-day felt experience of happiness did not.

What the Research Actually Says About Money and Happiness

Wealth building over a lifetime is not a project with a completion date. It is a practice: the sustained, evolving, occasionally disrupted but consistently re-established engagement with your financial life that produces, over decades, the compound result of thousands of small good decisions.

The long view is worth holding, not tightly as a source of pressure but lightly as a source of perspective. A difficult quarter in a twenty-year practice is a quarter. A year when the market declined and the investment account shrank is a year. The shortterm fluctuations that feel so significant in the moment are, from the perspective of the full arc, the ordinary texture of the journey rather than indicators of its direction.

The direction is determined by the consistency of the practice over the years, not by the performance of any individual period within them. Every week of the weekly review, every month of the automated contribution, every year of the annual strategic review adds to a compound that the individual periods are too small to see clearly. The navigator's position fix, taken each week, builds a record that only makes sense when read across many months. That record, in a few years, becomes the most motivating financial document most people have ever seen about themselves. Keep the practice. Return to it when it is disrupted. Hold the long view. The wealth is building.

4.2 What a Rich Life Actually Feels Like

Defining financial success in terms that are genuinely and specifically yours

"He is richest who is content with the least"

- *Socrates*

The question that most personal finance books never ask is the most important one.

Not how to invest. Not how to budget. Not how to negotiate. Those questions have answers that can be researched and implemented. The question that is almost never asked, because it does not have a researched answer and cannot be implemented by anyone else, is this: what does a financially successful life actually look and feel like for you, specifically?

Not the generic version. Not the cultural default of accumulating as much as possible for as long as possible, which is a goal that has no natural endpoint and therefore no experience of arrival. Not the social media version of early retirement and passive income and financial freedom, which describes a surface condition rather than a felt one. Your version. The specific texture of a financial life that, when you are living it, feels like genuine security and genuine freedom simultaneously.

This question matters practically because the motivation that sustains a financial practice over a lifetime must be connected to something real and specific. The practice driven by vague aspiration or competitive comparison tends to stall when the aspiration fades or the comparison produces discouragement. The practice driven by a specific, personally articulated vision of what becomes possible when the financial patterns have been addressed tends to endure, because the vision remains relevant even when the practice is difficult.

The Two Things Money Actually Provides

Strip away the surface complexity and money provides two things that matter deeply to human wellbeing. Security and optionality. Understanding the distinction between them is useful because they have different financial requirements and different timelines, and confusing them produces a financial plan that is imprecise about what it is trying to achieve.

Security is the condition in which your basic needs, shelter, food, healthcare, the maintenance of your household and the people in it, are met without ongoing anxiety about whether they will continue to be met. Security is not abundance. It is not having more than you need. It is the specific relief of knowing that the essential structure of your life is not under immediate threat, that an unexpected disruption will not produce a crisis, that the next month is already handled.

The research on the relationship between income and wellbeing is instructive here. Studies in multiple countries consistently find that wellbeing increases significantly with income up to a threshold that covers essential needs and a modest buffer above them, and then levels off. The professional who genuinely cannot meet their basic needs is significantly less happy than the professional who can. The billionaire is not significantly happier than the professional who is genuinely secure. What produces the largest wellbeing gain is the move from financial precarity to financial security. Above security, the returns diminish sharply.

Optionality is something different: the ability to make choices that would not be possible without a certain level of financial resources. The ability to consider a career change without being entirely constrained by immediate income requirements. The ability to take an extended leave without catastrophic financial consequence. The ability to decline work that conflicts with your values, or accept work that aligns with them even at a lower salary. The ability to help someone you love without it representing a genuine financial sacrifice. The ability to make decisions primarily on the basis of what you want rather than what you immediately need. Optionality is what the financial freedom conversation is actually about when it is about something real. It is the practical expression of the idea that money, beyond the security threshold, is a tool for enabling a life in which the important decisions are genuinely yours to make. Not all decisions, not the elimination of constraint, but meaningful expansion of the space within which your choices are real rather than dictated by circumstance.

Defining Your Enough

The most useful financial planning exercise I have encountered, and one that is almost entirely absent from conventional financial guidance, is the specific, honest articulation of what enough looks like for you.

Not as a net worth figure, though that can eventually be calculated. As a lived experience. What would your day look like if you had genuine financial security? What would you stop doing that you currently do because you feel financially compelled to? What would you start doing that you currently do not? What would the morning feel like? What would the relationship with your work feel like? What would the experience of an unexpected expense feel like?

These questions have different answers for different people, and the differences matter more than most financial planning frameworks acknowledge. For one person, enough means the certainty that their children's education is funded and their retirement is on a sound trajectory. For another, it means the ability to work part-time without financial penalty. For another, it means the freedom to pursue work that is intrinsically meaningful rather than financially optimal. For another, it means the capacity to support their parents without that support representing a choice between their family of origin and their family of creation.

None of these versions of enough is more legitimate than another. But they have substantially different financial requirements, different timelines, and different implications for what the financial practice should prioritise. The person whose enough is a funded education and a secure retirement is building toward something quite different from the person whose enough is the ability to leave a high-pressure role in three years. Both paths can be navigated intelligently. Neither can be navigated intelligently without knowing which path is actually being navigated.

Write your version of enough. Not the version that sounds most responsible or most ambitious or most aligned with what you think the answer should be. The honest version. What would be enough for you to feel that the financial practice had succeeded? What would be enough for you to feel that the wealth you had built was doing the work it was built for?

That definition is not a limitation on your ambition. It is the north star without which the financial practice has no specific destination and therefore no clear measure of progress. With it, every month of the Clarity Foundation review, every annual strategic review, every compensation conversation, has a specific orientation. You know what you are building toward. And knowing what you are building toward makes the building easier to sustain.

Wealth as a Relationship, Not an Endpoint

I want to close the main body of this book with a frame that has been implicit throughout and deserves to be made explicit, because it changes the felt experience of the entire financial practice.

Your relationship with money is a relationship. It has a history, formed by experiences you did not choose. It has patterns that developed before you were old enough to examine them. It has been shaped by people and cultures and circumstances that pre-date your conscious awareness of what you were absorbing from them. And like any relationship, it is not fixed. It can be examined and it can change. It responds to attention and to practice in the same way that any other significant relationship in your life responds to attention and practice.

A healthy relationship with money is not an obsessive one. The Vigilance Trapper's constant monitoring is not a healthy relationship with money any more than constant surveillance is a healthy relationship between people. It is not an avoidant one either. The Deferrer's studied non-engagement is not peace with money any more than never discussing a difficult subject is peace in a relationship. It is not a transactional one, in which money exists only as a means to purchases, with no relationship to the larger arc of a life being built deliberately.

A healthy relationship with money is honest, regular, forward-looking, and proportionate. You know where you stand. You engage with that reality on a consistent schedule rather than in crisis-driven episodes. You make decisions from information rather than from avoidance or anxiety. You understand what you are building and why. You can weather disruption without dismantling what has been built, and you can return to the practice after a disruption without requiring a perfect re-start.

You are capable of this relationship. The evidence of that capability is in the fact that you have read this far: that you brought enough honest interest and enough tolerance for discomfort to engage with what this book covers. That is the starting condition for everything. The practice builds on that starting condition, one week at a time, one annual review at a time, one conversation at a time.

The wealth is within reach. It has been all along. What this book has been about is closing the distance between you and it.

THE RECEIPT

"Not everything that counts can be counted, and not everything that can be counted counts"

- *William Bruce Cameron*

Here is a story that is specifically mine, because this book asked you for honesty and it would be dishonest not to offer some in return at the end as well as the beginning.

Some years ago, after a particularly demanding stretch at work, the kind where you spend more consecutive weeks in an absorbed professional intensity than you planned and where anything requiring sustained attention beyond the immediate becomes mentally scheduled for later, I realised I had not looked at my investment account in approximately four months.

Not four months without contributing. The contribution was automated and it had been running every month, undisturbed, without requiring anything from me. Four months without looking. Four months without knowing whether the balance had grown or fallen, whether the allocation was still appropriate, whether the practice I had built with some deliberate effort over the previous two years was doing what it was intended to do.

When I finally looked, with the slightly braced attention you bring to something you have been half-avoiding, what I found was unremarkable. The balance had grown. Not dramatically; the markets had been mixed. But it had grown, and the contributions had arrived faithfully each month, and the account was simply there, doing its patient, automated work, regardless of whether I had been paying attention or not.

What I felt in that moment was not pride in having done something clever. I had not done anything clever. I had set up a system at some earlier point and the system had run. What I felt was something closer to gratitude for the version of myself who had set up the system: the person who, in a moment of relative calm and clarity some time earlier, had made a specific decision that then operated quietly and reliably through the months of busyness that followed.

That is the promise of financial practice done well. Not the dramatic transformation. Not the spectacular return. Not the triumphant moment of arriving at some imagined financial destination. The quiet, reliable persistence of a system built during a calm moment, continuing to operate through the uncalm ones, compounding patiently in the background of a life that is too full and too real to attend to it every month.

Throughout the writing of this book, I spoke with people about their financial lives across different income levels, different industries, different countries, and different stages of life. The variety of specific situations was significant. The consistency of the core experience was striking.

Almost everyone, at some level, felt that they knew more than they were acting on. Almost everyone carried some version of the knowing-doing gap. Almost everyone had, rarely articulated but persistently felt, the sense that their financial life had not yet caught up with what they were capable of.

That sense is not a failing. It is an accurate observation about a specific gap between knowledge and pattern, and this book has been about closing it. The patterns that created the gap are visible now. They have names. Named patterns, held honestly rather than shamefully, can be changed through the accumulated practice of doing the specific things that contradict them.

The changes are available. The wealth is within reach. It has been for some time.

Begin today. Any step. One account looked at. One contribution automated. One sentence in the Evidence Journal. One breath before the next financial engagement.

The compound curve of financial growth is patient. It will work with whatever starting point you give it. The only starting point that produces no result is the one that never happens. That version of you is already sufficient. That step is already available. The compound curve of financial growth is patient enough to work with both.

The wealth within your reach is not waiting for a version of you that has everything sorted. It is waiting for the version of you who exists right now, with the patterns and the history and the imperfect relationship with money that you have been carrying, and who is willing to take one specific, small, concrete step in the right direction.

I tell you this not to present myself as a model of financial virtue, which I am not, but because the credibility of anything in this book rests on it having been tested against a real financial life rather than constructed from research alone.

The research is real and I have tried to represent it accurately. The personal dimension is equally real, and the combination of the two is what I hope gives this book the specific quality of usefulness that financial writing sometimes lacks: the recognition that the person writing it is not exempt from the patterns they are describing.

I used the three-breath reset before sitting down to write several of the chapters in Part Two, because the writing required me to examine patterns that I recognised in myself as well as describing them for the reader. The Evidence Journal that I recommend in Chapter Ten is one I have kept, inconsistently but genuinely, for several years.

The Annual Strategic Review that I describe in Chapter Twelve is a practice I have held on the same date each year for four years. The salary conversations that Chapter Fourteen describes are ones I have had, with the preparation framework I describe there, and they went better than the months of deferral that preceded each one suggested they would.

Writing this book required me to examine my own financial life with a level of honesty that I had been managing to avoid for some years. Not because the examination was catastrophic. It was not.

Because even a financial life that is broadly functional has specific gaps, specific deferrals, specific places where the pattern has been quietly costing more than it should, and looking at those places directly required the same physiological regulation I have been recommending throughout these pages.

THE 30-DAY WEALTH ACTIVATION PLAN

One action per day. Fifteen minutes or less. Starting tomorrow morning.

The sequence below follows the structure of the book: awareness first, foundation second, action third, architecture fourth. Do not skip ahead. Each week prepares the nervous system for the week that follows. Each action is designed to be completable in fifteen minutes or less, with a clear beginning and a clear end.

Week One: See Clearly

Day 1

Write your financial history in one page. Not your current numbers: the emotional story of money in your life growing up. What was said, and what was never said? What did money feel like in your household?

Day 2

Identify your primary Wealth Profile from Chapter Three. Write one sentence, honest and specific, about what that profile has cost you in the last three years.

Day 3

Begin your Evidence Journal. First entry: today's date, why you are starting, and one financial action from your past that you are genuinely proud of, however small.

Day 4

Practice the three-breath reset three times today, not connected to any financial task. Four counts in, six counts out. Learn the physical experience before you need it.

Day 5

Complete your Opportunity Audit from Chapter Four. All four sections. Write your personal opportunity total at the top of the page with today's date.

Day 6

Identify two or three money scripts from your family history. Write next to each one: is this still true in my current reality? What evidence do I have?

Day 7

Rest. Read back over what you wrote this week. Notice what surprised you. Write one sentence about what you will carry into next week.

Week Two: Build the Foundation

Day 8

Complete the Financial Inventory. Every account, every debt, every asset. Calculate your net worth. Write the figure with today's date. This is your starting line.

Day 9

Practice the three-breath reset and body scan before opening any financial account today. Then look at every account balance in one session. Make no decisions. Only observe.

Day 10

Map your current automation. What is already on automatic payment? What is not? List everything that could be automated and is not yet.

Day 11

Schedule your Weekly Financial Review: recurring, same day and time each week, in your calendar. Give it a name you will not find reasons to avoid. Day 12

Identify the interest rate on every debt you carry. Which is the most expensive? Calculate specifically what it is costing you annually.

Day 13

Write your personal Wealth Lock Loop as it operates in your life: your specific trigger, your specific block response, your specific disengagement behaviour, and your specific rebound pattern.

Day 14

Rest. Do something with no connection to money. Recovery is part of the practice, not a departure from it.

Week Three: Take Action

Day 15

Complete your first Weekly Financial Review using the full protocol from Chapter Ten. Three-breath reset first. Eight minutes of pure observation. One small action committed to. One sentence in the Evidence Journal.

Day 16

Set up one automation that does not yet exist: a savings transfer, a bill payment, or an investment contribution. Any amount. The automation is the goal, not the size.

Day 17

Make one extra payment, any amount above the minimum, on your highest-interest debt. Write it in the Evidence Journal.

Day 18

If you have no investment account: open one today. Any broadly appropriate index fund. If you do have one: log in, look at the balance, and write in the Evidence Journal that you looked and nothing catastrophic followed.

Day 19

Research your market compensation rate using at least two professional sources. Write down the median and the 75th percentile for your role, experience, and location.

Day 20

Make one proactive financial contact you have been deferring. Your bank, your insurance provider, your employer's benefits team. Ask one specific question.

Day 21

Write Evidence Journal entries for each of the six action days this week. Include what you did, what you expected or feared, and what actually happened.

Week Four: Build Forward

Day 22

Review your emergency reserve. What is its current balance? What would it cover? Set an automatic contribution to it if you have not already.

Day 23

Review the beneficiary designations on your accounts and insurance policies. Update any that are out of date. This takes twenty minutes and its value is disproportionate to its effort.

Day 24

Have one financial conversation you have been deferring, with a partner, a manager, or a creditor. Prepare it with the threebreath reset. Have it. Write about it afterward.

Day 25

Read back through your complete Evidence Journal from Day 3.

Write one paragraph about what has changed since you started.

Day 26

Write your personal definition of enough: not as a number but as a lived experience. What would your day feel like? What would you stop doing? What would you start?

Day 27

Identify the one action from this month that produced the most genuine sense of progress or relief. Make a plan to repeat it monthly.

Day 28

Draft your Annual Financial Review agenda for the coming year. Three to five specific financial improvements, each with a planned implementation date.

Day 29

Write your personal Wealth Resilience Protocol from Chapter Sixteen: who you will call in the first twenty-four hours of a financial shock, your regulation sequence, and your first action.

Day 30

Complete your second Weekly Financial Review. Compare your net worth today to your net worth on Day 8. Notice not only the number but what has changed in how the review feels to do. Write about it.

Thirty days. Not a transformation: a foundation. The weekly reviews continue. The automated contributions run. The annual strategic review lands on its date each year. The practice deepens. The thirty days described above are not a programme with a beginning and an end. They are the first thirty days of a practice that continues for the rest of your financial life. At Day 30, you will have two data points for your net worth, two completed weekly reviews, one automated contribution running, one debt addressed with an extra payment, one salary benchmark researched, one financial conversation had.

You will also have thirty days of Evidence Journal entries showing what you did, what you feared, and what actually happened. That journal, read from beginning to end on Day 30, is the most honest possible summary of what has changed. Read it. Then begin Day 31. Whatever the number says on Day 30: it is better than it would have been if you had not begun. The compound curve has started. It runs from today.

ABOUT THE AUTHOR

Suraj Raina has spent his career at the intersection of human behaviour and commercial performance.

As E-commerce and Regional Customer Development Manager at Kenvue, and in previous roles at Marico Limited, Perfetti Van Melle, and ITC Limited, he has spent more than a decade studying how people make decisions under pressure.

The fast-moving consumer goods environment is an unusually honest laboratory for human decision-making: the gap between understanding and action has direct, visible, commercial consequences, and the patterns of avoidance, deferral, and anxiety-driven behaviour that appear in personal financial life appear with similar regularity in professional commercial life.

The Wealth Within grew from that observation. Watching high-performing sales professionals and business owners make sharp decisions in their work and muddled ones in their own financial lives, consistently and across different companies and different markets, produced the central question this book addresses: why does the knowing-doing gap in personal finance persist despite adequate knowledge, and what specifically closes it?

The answer, developed through years of professional observation, extensive reading in behavioural economics and financial psychology, and the honest examination of his own financial patterns, is what you have just finished reading.

Suraj holds an MBA in Marketing from the Symbiosis Institute of Business Management, Bengaluru. He is also the author of FMCG Blueprint: Your No-Nonsense Guide to FMCG Success, a practical guide to the strategy and psychology of the fast-moving consumer goods industry, available on Amazon and at major booksellers.

He writes about consumer behaviour, decision-making under commercial pressure, and the psychology of professional performance.

His first book, FMCG Blueprint Series, addressed the professional knowledge gap in fast-moving consumer goods. This book addresses a different gap, in a domain that affects everyone who earns a salary and has not yet fully claimed what that salary makes possible. He considers the second book the more personally consequential of the two.

The Wealth Within is the direct result of turning the lens of his professional expertise on his own financial behaviour and, eventually, on the financial behaviour he had observed across thousands of professional interactions over a decade.

The frameworks in this book are not theoretical constructs. They are the output of that specific combination of professional observation and personal examination, tested against the reality of an actual financial life rather than constructed in the abstract.

What drew him to write this particular book was a question that his professional background made it impossible to ignore. In consumer goods, the gap between stated preference and revealed preference, between what people say they will do and what they actually do, is the most commercially important territory in the industry.

Understanding that gap is how brands are built and how markets are won. Suraj spent years studying it professionally. Then, long enough into his career to have no excuse for the oversight, he noticed he had been living a version of it in his own financial life: knowing what he should be doing and not doing it, for reasons that turned out to be specific, understandable, and addressable rather than general, shameful, and fixed.

Connect: linkedin.com/in/surajraina06

NOTES AND FURTHER READING

The following works directly informed the research, frameworks, and arguments in this book. They are grouped by theme rather than order of appearance, as most of them speak to multiple chapters simultaneously. All are recommended for readers who want to go deeper on any of the core subjects. They are grouped by theme rather than order of appearance because most speak to multiple chapters, and any one of them will reward the time spent with it.

On Behavioural Finance and Financial Decision Making

Housel, Morgan. The Psychology of Money. Harriman House, 2020. The essential modern work on how emotional and psychological factors shape financial outcomes. Ronald Read's story in the Introduction is drawn from this book.

Kahneman, Daniel. Thinking, Fast and Slow. Farrar, Straus and Giroux, 2011. The foundational text on System One and System Two thinking, extensively referenced in Chapter Two.

Thaler, Richard H. and Cass R. Sunstein. Nudge. Yale University Press, 2008. The theoretical foundation for the automation emphasis throughout Part Three, and for the account-naming practice in Chapter Twelve.

Mullainathan, Sendhil and Eldar Shafir. Scarcity. Times Books, 2013. The cognitive bandwidth research discussed in Chapter Two. Among the most important books on the relationship between financial stress and decision quality.

Ariely, Dan. Predictably Irrational. HarperCollins, 2008. Accessible and well-researched on the systematic irrationalities that govern human financial behaviour.

On Money Scripts and Financial Psychology

Klontz, Brad and Ted Klontz. Mind Over Money. Crown Business, 2009. The origin of the money script framework discussed in Chapter Seven. The four categories of money script are drawn from their clinical research.

Newcomb, Sarah. Loaded: Money, Psychology, and How to Get Ahead Without Leaving Your Values Behind. Wiley, 2016. An underread but excellent examination of the psychological dimensions of financial behaviour.

Babcock, Linda and Sara Laschever. Women Don't Ask. Princeton University Press, 2003. The foundational research on salary negotiation referenced in Chapter Fourteen.

On Habit Formation and Behaviour Change

Clear, James. Atomic Habits. Avery, 2018. The most practically useful book on habit formation available. The principles of identitybased habits and the aggregation of marginal gains are central to Chapters Eleven and Twelve.

Fogg, BJ. Tiny Habits. Houghton Mifflin Harcourt, 2019. The motivation wave concept and the principle of making new behaviours as small as possible are drawn from Fogg's research.

Duhigg, Charles. The Power of Habit. Random House, 2012. On the structure of habit loops and the specific mechanism by which they can be changed.

Dweck, Carol S. Mindset. Random House, 2006. On the growth mindset that underlies the shift from identity statements to behavioural descriptions throughout this book.

On the Neuroscience of Stress and Financial Behaviour

Van der Kolk, Bessel. The Body Keeps the Score. Viking, 2014. Essential background for Chapter Six on the body's role in financial anxiety and the somatic practices that address it.

Sapolsky, Robert M. Why Zebras Don't Get Ulcers. Henry Holt, 2004. The definitive accessible work on the biology of stress and its effects on cognition and decision-making. The cortisol research in Chapter Two is informed by Sapolsky's work.

Damasio, Antonio. Descartes' Error. Putnam, 1994. The research on emotion and decision-making that opens Chapter Six.

On Shame, Vulnerability, and Sustained Change

Brown, Brene. Daring Greatly. Gotham Books, 2012. The shame and vulnerability research that informs the shame amplifier discussion in Chapter Five and the compassionate framing throughout the book.

Neff, Kristin. Self-Compassion. William Morrow, 2011. On the role of self-compassion in sustained behaviour change, directly relevant to the relapse discussion in Chapter Sixteen.

On Personal Finance Practice

Housel, Morgan. Same as Ever. Harriman House, 2023. On the enduring patterns of human behaviour in financial markets and economic history.

Perkins, Bill. Die with Zero. Mariner Books, 2020. A useful reframe of wealth accumulation as a means to lived experience rather than an end in itself. Relevant to the 'defining your enough' discussion in Chapter Seventeen.

Sethi, Ramit. I Will Teach You to Be Rich. Workman Publishing, 2009. Practical, automation-focused personal finance advice for the earlier stages of wealth building.

BY THE AUTHOR

Raina, Suraj. FMCG Blueprint (2025) and FMCG Blueprint 2.0 – The Operator's Edition (2026). The author's previous book on the strategy, psychology, and mechanics of the fast-moving consumer goods industry. Available on Amazon.

THE WEALTH WITHIN: How to Unlock the Hidden Fortune Your Mind Has Been Holding Back

A note on how to use this reading list: these books are not prerequisites for implementing what The Wealth Within describes. The practices in Part Three can be begun before any of the above has been read. The reading list is for the reader who wants to understand more deeply the science behind a practice they have already started, or who finds that a particular chapter resonated and wants to follow the thread further. Start with Housel if you read only one. Start with Clear if the habit formation chapters were most useful. Start with van der Kolk if Chapter Six changed how you understand your own responses to money. Each of these books will return the time you spend with it.

Suraj Raina: linkedin.com/in/surajraina06

One hour per week. Twelve months. The beginning of something that compounds.

www.ingramcontent.com/pod-product-compliance
Lightning Source LLC
LaVergne TN
LVHW100315210926
848480LV00003B/1128

* 9 7 9 8 9 0 4 7 9 4 4 7 7 *